FLY TYING
WITH SYNTHETICS
Patterns & Techniques

FLY TYING
WITH SYNTHETICS
Patterns & Techniques

by Phil Camera

Illustrated by Don Puterbaugh
Photography by Tim Savard & G. Anderson
Color Plates by Gordon Anderson

SWAN·HILL
PRESS

Copyright © 1992 Phil Camera

First published in the UK in 1992
by Swan Hill Press
an imprint of Airlife Publishing Ltd.

Published simultaneously in the USA by Voyageur Press Inc.

British Library Cataloguing in Publication Data

A catalogue record of this book is available from the British Library

ISBN 1 85310 338 1

Produced by Specialty Book Marketing Inc. and designed by Studio 31

Printed in Singapore by Kyodo Printing Co. (S'pore) pte Ltd.

Swan Hill Press

An imprint of Airlife Publishing Ltd.
101 Longden Road, Shrewsbury SY3 9EB, England.

Table of Contents

FOREWORD

I don't really remember when Phil Camera and I met each other, or when we became friends. We both do a lot of demonstration fly tying, so I gradually got to know the fellow demonstrating the Larva Lace material at the center of the biggest crowd in the place. Sometimes, I found myself in the crowd watching his techniques and learning something new and useful to my own fly tying. You have to listen carefully and watch closely because Phil speaks in a soft voice as he explains techniques he makes things look easy. You'll find, however, they aren't as simple as they looked when you get back to your vise.

Part of what makes Phil such an exceptional teacher is that he has infinite patience. As he explains something to you, he looks you right in the eye, giving each student the impression that this seminar was set up just for him. This is a rare gift in a teacher.

No question is without merit to Phil, and no fly tyer who has something he would like to learn from Phil is sent away empty handed.

In *FLY TYING WITH SYNTHETICS – PATTERNS AND TECHNIQUES* you will learn something else about Phil. He doesn't keep any flytying secrets to himself. I know a lot of big name professional fly tyers who are like chefs with recipes they share, managing to leave out a couple of key ingredients. This keeps anyone else from quite duplicating the original recipe. You'll find that Phil will give all of the pieces essential for tying any of the patterns included.

It's indeed a shame that most of you who'll use this book will not get the chance to sit down and tie with Phil Camera. As a dentist and professional fly tyer, I can't help but notice how a person works and how they use their hands. Phil sits at his vise with his materials scattered helter-skelter about him on the table, on chairs, and even on the floor. He looks up at you from under heavy lidded eyes and says, "now, watch this." Short, fat fingers which you feel can't possibly be graceful or dexterous take up the bobbin and move the thread to the vise, and what you see him do makes you think of Van Cliburn at the piano. I once heard it said "the hands can't perform what the mind cannot conceive." Obviously Phil's mind is up to the task. He is an innovative and masterful fly tyer.

Every time I talk with Phil, I have to ask him again what it is he does professionally other than his fly tying related activities. Grinning, he patiently explains (for the hundredth time) that he was, up until recently, in the Civil Service employed at the Air Force Academy's M.W.R. branch to manage their 650 acre outdoor recreational facility, complete with stream and several ponds . . . all of which had trout. Among his duties were the coordinating and teaching of fly fishing and fly tying courses. I know all this of course, because I have known Phil for quite some time. Presently Phil is working full-time in pursuit of developing and marketing of new products for Phil's Tackle-Larva

Lace Products™ in Woodland Park CO. I guess I still can't believe anyone could have been that lucky. I'm certainly old enough to know that the grass is always greener on the other side of the fence and that there must have been downsides to Phil's job. What they were, however, I cannot for the life of me imagine.

Certainly there are few people as qualified to take on the task of writing this book. You'll find some unique and useful ideas between its pages, and it will be a book which will sit open beside your vise many a night. My favorite fly tying books are those which despite my care, end up spotted with errant drops of tying cement and bits of feather between the pages. I'll bet a jungle cock cape that *FLY TYING WITH SYNTHETICS – PATTERNS AND TECHNIQUES* will be handed on to my grandchildren in just that condition.

Dr. Eric Pettine
Ft. Collins, Colorado

DEDICATION

This book is dedicated to you, the tyers who will use it. It is written with the hope you will pick up one small, new piece of tying information or that you will be stimulated to try something you've never tried (*or tied*) before.

To the many fine people who have fished with me and attended my clinics who have urged me to put this all down on paper, I thank you one and all for your encouragement and inspiration.

I hope you find in this book something to experiment with and that these innovations in the art of fly tying help keep you smarter than the fish.

Phil
December 1991

ACKNOWLEDGEMENTS

Since this is the first book I've ever written, it goes without saying that there was an army of people behind the scenes. Without all of these people I never would have reached this point. I am bound to forget somebody, so if you are one of those, please accept my humble apologies.

Thanks to Harold Sessa of New Haven Connecticut, without whom I would never have met my publisher, Bill Corsa. Bill, your patience with me has been more than appreciated. Thank you for the opportunity to work with Specialty Book Marketing.

Dr. Eric Pettine for contributing the Forward to this book. Eric! Haven't you ever seen a crab missing one leg? Thank you, Eric.

Poul Jorgenson for being the first person to recognize Larva Lace on a national level. Thank you, Poul, for the many Larva Lace patterns in your book, *COMPLETE FLY TYING*.

Skip Camera, my son, whom without his help there would be no book.

George Gehrke if it hadn't been for you, I may never have followed through to this point in my fly tying career.

Don Puterbaugh, a friend and fine artist and tyer who didn't even hesitate in offering his illustrations to this book.

Bill Blackstone, for contributing the Introduction to Tying Techniques, thank you.

Chuck Rizutto of Farmington, New Mexico who tested Larva Lace patterns.

Dave Stark of Woodland Park, Colorado. Thanks for working so hard in the many things you have done to help me complete this book.

Jason Volmer Colorado Springs, for testing Larva Lace patterns.

John Gross, from the Lure Flash company in Yorkshire, England, for your help and contribution to this book and the synthetic fly tying world.

Robert Ransom of Fairfax, California, thank you for the definitive description of Fender Flies.

Illustrations by Don Puterbaugh of Salida,CO, Author of *Basic Fly Tying, Fly Fisherman's Primer, Expert Fly Tying,* and numerous articles for national fishing periodicals.

Black and White Photography by Tim Savard of Concord, New Hampshire, thanks Tim for our black & white photos and great company on the South Platte.

Cover Photography — Bob Frantz, Woodland Park, Colorado

Acknowledgement of Material Suppliers who sent samples for testing

Flyrite
LureFlash
Mill Stream Products
Kreinik Fly Tying Materials
Renzetti Fly Tying Tools
Larva Lace Products
Uni-Thread

Contributing fly tyers

Greg Asbury – Gunnison, Colorado
Jerry Berg (Dr. Fly) – Denver, Colorado
Phil Camera – Woodland Park, Colorado
Frank Marcotte – Salt Lake City, Utah
Rick Murphy – Colorado Springs, Colorado
Angelo Musiani – Bologna, Italy
Bob Popovics – Sea Park, New Jersey
Don Puterbaugh – Salida, Colorado
Rob Ransom – Fairfax, California
Roy Richardson – Westminster, California
Chuck Rizzuto – Farmington, New Mexico
Larry Walker – Denver, Colorado
George Watkins – Colorado Springs, Colorado
Jason Volmer – Colorado Springs, Colorado

INTRODUCTION

As we go down the road of fly tying, we continually see new flies and innovative patterns. However, one of the most exciting parts of this journey is the occasional arrival of new materials. By new materials I mean synthetics, man made substances. Without question, these materials are giving us an opportunity to add innovative patterns to our gallery of flies. They are also giving us the opportunity to step back and re-evaluate many of our older patterns, giving them something of a face lift, and even broadening their fish producing capabilities.

The creations that emerge from a fly tyer's vise are often his personal rendition of an existing pattern, or his interpretation of some aquatic food source. Some flies are even tied as a tool to provoke the fish, placing most flies into one of three categories.

1. Duplication
2. Simulation
3. Attraction

Some folks believe these categories should be obtained through fur and feather only. Right or wrong, synthetics are here to stay. My aim in this book is to introduce some of the many synthetics used in fly tying as well as new techniques used when tying with these materials.

Literally volumes could be written on this subject, however as you proceed through this book, you will find that most of the techniques we use when tying with synthetics are the same that have been used for many years. We need to continue the old and adopt new techniques when working with more modern materials, always remembering the importance of natural furs and feathers.

You will find many pictures of completed flies with a reference code. This will enable you to relate to a finished fly while learning a technique. Many of the patterns you'll see will be older classics with only slight variations using some of the more modern materials.

GLOSSARY OF
SYNTHETIC MATERIALS

ANGORA YARN: Made in France, this is a coarse yarn made of angora rabbit fur.

ANTRON: Translucent synthetic fibers used in flosses and yarns to produce a high sparkle effect.

BEAD CHAIN: Silver or brass chain sold as pull chain for electrical items. Perfect for use as eyes for a large variety of wet flys simply by cutting the beads off the chain.

PLASTIC BEAD CHAIN: Similar in appearance to brass or gold chain. Primarily used for patterns requiring large attracting eyes with minimal weight.

BODY GLASS: Plastic type ribbing material solid in construction.

BURNT MONO: Monofiliment burned creating a ball on the end.

CHENILLE: Chenille is similar to a pipe cleaner in appearance but has a soft fabric core instead of a rigid wire core. It is used mostly when tying large wet fly and nymph patterns. Traditionally, chenille has been available in three sizes; small, medium and large. However, in the past few years there have been a number of newer materials falling under the chenille category.

ULTRA CHENILLE: Similar to chenille except with a thicker material appearance. Ultra chenille looks like a fuzzy string. This small size chenille comes in a large variety of colors and can be purchased in most fly fishing shops and catalog houses. Ultra chenille is the main ingredient for the recently created San Juan worm.

SUPER MICRO CHENILLE: Super Micro chenille is even smaller and gives the appearance of a piece of thin suede string. This material is presently being imported from Italy. Micro chenille gives you the ability to tie very small nymphs and lends itself to weaving quite well.

CRYSTAL CHENILLE: Crystal chenille is a chenille-like product made of mylar tinsel. It has a fine fabric core and fine mylar pieces projecting from its sides approximately $1/4''$. This is very similar to the garlands that you decorate your Christmas tree with, except in a much smaller size.

SPARKLE CHENILLE: Identical to crystal chenille, but identified as a manufacturer's name brand.

CRYSTAL HAIR: A very fine stripped mylar with a drill bit type twist permanently set in the material. This material gives off a sparkling effect as the light reflects when hitting each twist. Available in a large variety of colors.

CRYSTAL YARN: Very similar to crystal chenille, but offered by a different distributor. Crystal yarn is becoming very popular when tying attractor patterns such as those used in salt water and Steelhead.

DOLL EYES: Small plastic eyes with movable black pupil. these eyes are normally used on large popping bugs or bass and saltwater patterns.

ELASTIC FIBER: Used as rubber legs and antennas for attracting patterns. Can be purchased in most fly shops as a 1″ wide strip of rubber. When stretched and snapped back, the material will separate into tiny strands. Available in a variety of colors.

ESTAZ: Estaz is a product of Glissen Gloss™, producers of Fantasy Flosses for creative needle arts. Very similar to Crystal Yarn, except that the mylar fringes extend from one side of the fabric core rather than a cylindrical pattern as with the yarn.

EVAZOTE: A commercial brand name high grade closed cell foam. Used primarily for dry flies and popping bugs.

FIB-ETTS: Very thin tapered synthetic fibers used as tails for dry flies. Similar to the fibers of a high grade artist's paint brush. Available in a variety of colors.

FISH FUZZ: Fish Fuzz is Nylon imitation fur. It is available in over 20 colors and gives a lifelike effect when in the water. Manufactured by Gerhke Products.

FISH HAIR: This is a synthetic hair used for tying large streamers, salt water flies, and bucktail lures. Fish hair is available in over 20 colors and three grades of coarseness:

    24 Denier – Light Hair
    50 Denier –Special Hair (ideal for dressing fresh water lead heads)
    70 Denier – Best for Large streamers and saltwater

FLOSS: Floss is a silk or rayon strand material. This material is used primarily for under body and external body areas. Floss is available in a large variety of colors and comes in 3 sizes. Single strand, double strand and four strand. When tying very small flies the multi-strand material can be separated and a fine textured single strand can be used. Make sure this material is flat and not twisted before tying. If the floss is twisted you will get an uneven build up.

    DANVILLE – U.S. Producer of fly tying floss
    UNI PRODUCTS – Canadian producer of fly tying floss

RAYON FLOSS: Floss is used for shiny fly bodies. It is available in at least 18 different colors.

FLY RITE: Fly Rite is a polypropylene dubbing. The availability of a large spectrum of colors and its tyer-friendly nature has made this material very popular among dry fly tyers. Polypropylene is used for dry flys because this synthetic fiber will not absorb water.

FLY SHEET: Fly sheet is a synthetic wing material. The material is very thin, but sturdy and the colored patterns on the material are truly convincing.

FRIZZ: Frizz is another variation of crystal yarn, but has extra long fringes.

FURRY FOAM: This is a flocked foam material. It can be used, when cut very thin, for wrapping of nymph bodies. This truly unique item comes in a variety of colors.

HARE-TRON: A synthetic antron dubbing material.

IMITATION FERN: Found in the imitation flower department of most any department store. the petals on these ferns are made of nylon and silk and can be used for wings or wing pads in a variety of patterns.

KEVLAR: An aerospace fiber stronger than nylon, developed and trademarked by Dupont Corporation.

KRYSTAL FLASH: Very similar to crystal hair, but produced by a different manufacturer.

LACE WING: Soft plasticized fine durable lace material suitable for realistic insect wings.

LARVA LACE® BODY MATERIAL: Larva Lace Body Material is a hollow, tubular vinyl material. This material is very soft and has a high elasticity factor (it stretches). Although primarily used for wet flies, you will see some dry fly patterns for it in this book. The most unique feature of this material is its hollow translucent construction. This makes Larva Lace Body Material the most versatile synthetic material available to the fly tyer today. As you read through this book, pick out the many applications and techniques available to you when tying with this unique material.

LARVA LACE® CLOSED CELL FLY TYING FOAM (evazote): A high grade closed cell foam. Available in solid sheets $3/16''$ thick and in sheets $1/16''$ with $1/8''$ pre-cut strips. Colors available are: black, white, yellow, orange, green, olive, red, blue and grey.

LARVA LACE® OPEN CELL FLY TYING FOAM: This is an open cell poly foam available in sheets of pre-cut strips. Used primarily for underbodies and tapering bodies of wet flies.

LARVA LACE® MIDGE LACE: Same as Larva Lace® Body Material but smaller in diameter, designed for fly sizes 18-26.

LARVA LACE® NYMPH RIB: Larva Lace® Nymph Rib is a half-round solid constructed ribbing material. Its solid design gives it a more exaggerated ribbing effect than the body material. It pulls down in size so that you can conventionally wrap flys in the size 20 range. Nymph rib is also translucent in appearance, and very soft.

LARVA LACE® TRANSLUCENT THREAD: Larva Lace® translucent thread is a fine diameter nylon thread. This thread is used when superior strength is needed with a very fine diameter. Translucent thread comes in two sizes ultra fine and fine as well as clear and translucent smoke. The ultra fine size is equivalent to the standard 6/0 thread in size but much stronger. Many people call this invisible thread and use it for ribbing or tying down other translucent material. The fly body will remain translucent without exposing the thread. You can also use the clear thread as an overbody protection when tying 18-24 size crystal emergers.

LATEX: Latex is a premium quality rubber. When used as fly tying material we find it mostly on bodies and wing cases. This material comes in medium, light-heavy and extra-heavy sheets measuring 5″ square. Cream, grey and green are the colors most commonly available however the cream color pantones very well giving you most any color you need. **Warning !!** Although this material is easy to work with and gives a very nice appearance it is extremely vulnerable to ultraviolet rays. To help prevent your fly from deteriorating in the sun light, you may want to coat the exposed latex areas with head cement.

LEAD EYES: Small hourglass shaped lead pieces used for weighting and attraction for wet flies requiring large eyes. Available chromed or standard lead grey color.

    Size 1 : Diam. 3mm, wt. .45 grams
    Size 2 : Diam. 4mm, wt. .90 grams
    Size 3 : Diam. 5.5mm, wt. 1.89 grams

LEAD TAPE: Thin rolled lead with an adhesive backing. Used to fold over a hook to form bodies on large streamers or other wet flies.

LED™: Although designed as a leader lead, LED has found its way onto many a fly tyers bench. This flat rolled lead is 3/32 wide and 4 feet long. Many tyers of large salt water and Alaskan patterns use this flat lead when pre-weighting their flys. Any amount can be used since it leaves an even flat surface over the shank of the hook.

LIGGAS: Polypropelene dubbing material.

LUREFLASH TWINKLE: This is a British product which has gained great popularity in the U.S. Twinkle is a single strand of pearl mobile intermingled and woven with 5 supporting strands of colored micro monofiliments. Effective as fly wings and bodies requiring only a slight flashing twinkle.

LUREFLASH PEARL FRONDZ: A mother of pearl chenille type material with long pearl fibers which pulsate with movement in the water.

LUREFLASH FLAT PEARL MYLAR: Available on spools $1/32''$, $1/16''$ and $3/32$ wide. Used to provide flashy appearance on nymphs and streamers.

LUREFLASH TRANSLUCENT: Long, thin mylar strips colored in translucent shades. Available in a large variety of colors.

LUREFLASH MOBILE: Metalized plastic flashing material similar to Flashabou.

METALLIC TINSEL: A very fine metal fiber wrapped around a fabric core. Used primarily for ribbing. Available in many sizes and colors.

MONOCORD: A heavy fly tying thread.

MONOFILIMENT: Nylon line used for tying thread, ribbing, or as a protective overwrap.

NYLON MESH: (Pantyhose) Used for reinforcement of the underside of feathers.

MYLAR TUBING: This is a braided, non-tarnishable Mylar. It's criss-cross appearance imitates the scales of a small fish. It is available in 3 sizes and a wide variety of colors, including fluorescents.

PANTONE: See permanant marking pen.

PEARL BODY FILM SHEET: Pearlized tinsel in oyster and mother of pearl. Available in 25mm wide sheets to enable the creative fly tyer to cut long strips to any desired size or shape.

PERMANENT MARKING PEN: High grade permanent felt tip pens used to color and shade many fly bodies or wings. Also used for making eyes on some patterns or coloring head areas.

PLASTIZOTE: High grade closed cell foam primarily used for dry fly patterns.

POLY FLASH: A rough ribbon texture with silver or gold color coating. Very durable overwrap body material.

POLY YARN: A yarn made of polypropelene, a synthetic material that will not absorb water. Poly yarn is used as a dubbing material as well as for making glo-bug or egg patterns. Available in a wide variety of colors.

POM-POMS: Small fabric balls available in many sizes and colors. Used as pre-made glo-bugs or eggs.

PRISM TAPE: Tape with an adhesive backing and highly reflective patterns on the exposed side. Available in a variety of colors.

PRISM TAPE EYES: Pre-cut small diameter circles of prism tape with black dot in the center. These eyes have a pull-off backing and can be applied to streamers and bass flies by just sticking them on with finger pressure.

RAFFIA: Made from the leaves of a palm tree used to make fly bodies and wing cases.

REFLECTOR FOIL: Squared metalized plastic sheet which has an adhesive back. It is available in silver, gold, red, blue, green, copper, and Mother of Pearl.

RUBBER LEGS: Very fine elastic strands used for legs on large patterns.

SEAL-X: This is a synthetic dubbing used to represent natural seal fur. Coarse in texture, great for many nymphs. Available in variety of colors.

SEQUINS: A small metal or plastic disc strung together used for fabric decoration. Gives a flashy scale appearance

SPARKLE GLITTER: Tiny reflecting particles used to mix in with clear epoxies or clear rubber cement. Available at most craft stores.

SPARKLE FLASH: A tough, super-reflective non-matting material. Similar to Flashabou, but cut in very fine strands. Made in Australia.

SPARKLE TWIST: An Australian product, basically a metallic tinsel offered in strands rather than on a spool.

SPARKLE YARN: A dyed yarn with a slight metallic surface of two criss-crossed silver filaments, providing a double ribbed effect. Ideal for obtaining increased attraction to the fly.

STREAMER HAIR: Long fiber synthetic hair used for jigs and streamers. Supplied by Wapsi.

SWANNUNDAZE: Swannundaze is a solid nylon ribbing material. The material was one of the very first plastic type ribbing materials available and dates back at least 20 years.

SWISS STRAW: A synthetic imitation of Raffia that is used for Nymphs and mayfly bodies.

SYNTHETIC DUBBING: A non natural material generally used in dry flies designed for its light gathering, texture and floatability.

TWIN LEAD EYES: See lead eyes.

TWISTED TINSEL: An all metal tinsel twisted around a nylon thread.

ULTRA HAIR: A synthetic hair that has tiny bends in the fiber. Excellent for large streamers and durability.

VINYL PAINT: Used when painting jigs and streamer eyes, as well as when painting plastic materials.

Z-LON: A synthetic wing and body material which offers a high sparkle quality.

Tying
Techniques

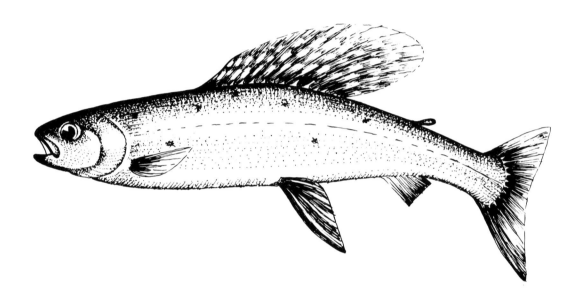

INTRODUCTION TO TYING TECHNIQUES

by Bill Blackstone

When Phil asked me to consider contributing some words to this book, he didn't have to ask twice, I jumped at the chance. One thing that has literally taken over my world of fly tying is the synthetic materials. I find myself seizing any opportunity available to advance the cause.

The world outside of feathers and furs can extend your interest and tying techniques to a new high without sacrificing any of the special effects you were trying to achieve. I certainly do not have a problem with feathers and furs. However, when hackles went from ten to eighty dollars in a period of ten years, I was soon searching for alternate sources.

Think about what you may be tying with synthetics right now without realizing it. Practically all dubbing today is synthetic. Most of the thread, tinsel, chenille and floss is man made. We used to have only silk for thread and floss. It lost color, was tough to control and certainly was not as strong as the thread today. Head cement was in the eighteenth century relative to design. Believe me, if the "good old days" were here again, most of you would give up tying.

Thought! Thought is the only requirement for use of synthetics. When you want to tie a pattern and you go to your fly shop, catalog, or reference book, evaluate each material for the possibility of substituting another product.

I think my first step over the line was to use poly yarn as a substitute for kip. One of the most common products we use is calf tail. The variance in this one product is so great it will drive a tyer crazy. Try tying an H&L Variant in a size eighteen and find an acceptable calf hair. If you don't use a synthetic, you are putting yourself through more pain than you realize. The best part is-the fish really do not care. Royal Wulff's in sixteen and eighteen sizes certainly go much better and faster with poly wings. And again, the fish do not care. How many quill wings do you fish with today? Admit it! You don't need them and neither do the fish. Products like Flash-a-bou, Larva Lace, Swannundaze, Crystal Hair, etc. are far more attractive, durable and easy to work with. A Caddis larva can be produced much better with synthetics.

Synthetics produce a more attractive fly. Every tyer wants to produce the fly that is most attractive to the fish.

Seining the water, turning over rocks, observing stream life is both rewarding and enlightening. Fishing over water with no takes is an experience we would all hope to avoid. Keeping a record of failures and success will refresh your memory when you return to that stream.

I fish in the Western Sierra's a great deal. While turning rocks and observing hatches, I noticed that the Mayflies in this area were close to hatching when the wing pads were dark. I took a standard Hair's Ear Nymph which was producing and tied a small piece of black plastic trash bag over the back of the thorax. I immediately increased my take. Thinking that I may have overstated my belief, I fished the original pattern over the same area followed by the modified fly and again increased my take. I tried it at different times and different places, with the same results. I then decided to try a legging system rather than the shaggy dubbing. After several trials, I used Hungarian Partridge neck feathers because of the mottled coloring. Again my take was increased. I continued to observe the hatch feeding habits. Large fish were consistently feeding in the film, making splashy rises. I constructed a seine of fine mesh screen and set about trying to study the available food, in what condition and configuration it was occurring.

In my sampling I observed a great many bugs in the process of hatching that left the dun and nymphal shuck together. It was a hunch on my part that the struggle in which these insects were involved while trying to shed their shucks, was attracting fish attention and giving a movement on which to focus. Armed with the patience to try another step, I added one last feature. Along with the black trash bag strip as a wing pad, the legging system, I now added a tuft of opaque clear plastic peeking out through a slit in the back of the trash bag that simulated a wing. Success! I attracted the larger fish.

This long-winded scenario is merely an example of the reasons I am convinced that synthetics are effective and feasible. Some say that this kind of fly tying falls into the "Duplication" category.

I fish Silver Creek in Idaho on occasion. This stream promotes possibly the finest and most prolific spinner fall a fisherman can experience. Activity like this can really try a fisherman's technique and patience. It does provide the angler with a perfect forum for observing fish feeding habits. The best pattern I have used to date is an all synthetic fly which I call a Poly-foam Spinner. It is easy to tie, floats beautifully and is a "duplicate" for the spinner.

Place a number nine sewing needle in the vise. Start wrapping near the tip with 6/0 thread. Use just enough to tie down the thread. Select two or three tail bristles, depending on pattern, secure them to the needle. Use either microfibits or bristles from a Simmons White Sable Paint Brush. Wrap the thread to the tip. On this pattern less winds are better. Select a 3/8″ strip of poly 2Dfoam about 1″ long and cut at a forty-five degree angle at one end forming a point in the middle.

Fold the poly-foam over the needle and wind the thread over the tip and then wrap the thread to the left palmering or ribbing the body. This creates the body segmentation effect. Form a whip finish using only two or three wraps and trim the thread long. (About 1″) Apply a small amount of head cement to the tip of the tail where the tail fibers come out. Spread the fibers apart allowing the head cement to set just momentarily. With thumb and forefinger grasp the base of the body that was ship finished, slide the body off the tip of the needle. There is the body.

Remove the needle from the vise and exchange it with an egg or short shank hook. Secure the body to the hook and trim off the excess. Select light yellow synthetic dubbing. Wrap a couple of winds over the base of the trimmed body. Use a clear 6 mil vinyl plastic bag material for wings. Fold in half, cut a wing profile suitable for the size mayfly being tied. Lay the wings flat on the hook and begin wrapping using a figure eight to secure the wing. Finish the head and whip finish. If the pattern is size twelve or above, use the same tail material under the fly at the head to form a legging system. Two fibers are all right, splay them. This will help break the aerodynamic problem of the wings.

The foam comes from the trash can. Every Electronics manufacturer uses this sheet foam to pack their units for shipping. Radio Shack and Circuit City throw away tons of it.

Tie everything in white or light colors. The light yellow or primrose color thread accepts the marker color faster than the poly. This enhances the segmented look.

I could go on and on with my "Love synthetics" song. The bottom line is that they are here, they are available at a fraction of the cost of most feathers and furs. They will extend your techniques. All it takes is experimentation. Next time you sit at your vise, try something new. Who knows? You may just discover a whole new world of tying.

SLIP OVER TECHNIQUE
WITH MYLAR TUBING

The slip over technique of fly tying lends itself only to tubular constructed materials. The most popular materials currently used are mylar tubular piping and Larva Lace body material.

Mylar tubing is most generally used when tying streamer patterns because of its fish scale like appearance. Its woven construction also gives it the ability to stretch when being slipped over a formed body. One of the easiest patterns to become familiar with mylar tubing is as follows:

MILTS'S SMELT

Materials:
Hook: Mustad 9674
Thread: 6/0 Uni-thread
Tail: Marabou
Underbody: Open cell foam
Overbody: Tubular mylar
Eye: Paint or stick on

Step 1. Tie in Marabou tail

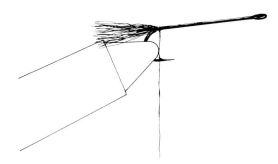

Step 2. Tie in a strip of open cell foam leaving the thread forward just behind the hook eye.

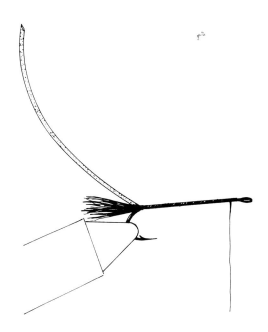

Step 3. Wrap the open cell foam forward building a taper. Make sure the tapered body is smaller than the inner diameter of the tubing.

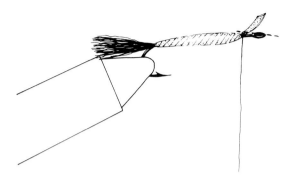

Step 4. Tie off the foam leaving the thread at the front end of the fly.

Step 5. Cut a strip of mylar tubing, remembering that you will need extra materials for your tie in area (approximately 1/8″).

Step 6. Fray the ends of the mylar tubing back approximately 1/8″.

Step 7. Slip the mylar tubing over the eye to where you tied off the foam underbody.

Step 8. Now tie down the frayed ends of the mylar, making sure that you tie back to where the fraying ends.

Step 9. Whip finish and wrap your thread to the rear of the fly.

Step 10. Fold back the mylar tubing by pushing the hook and formed body forward while holding the mylar with the opposite hand. (You are folding the tubing inside out.)

Step 11. Tie off the frayed mylar at the tail.

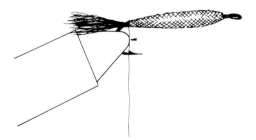

Step 12. Whip finish and remove thread.

Step 13. Shade the top surface of the fly with a Permanent marking pen using the color and shade closest to the fly you want to represent.

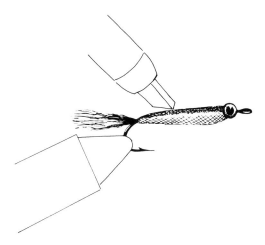

Step 14. Apply hard clear lacquer to the exposed thread and head section.

Step 15. Paint on eyes or use stick-ons. If stick-on eyes are used, lacquer over the eyes to insure that they won't fall off.

The technique of folding back the mylar in Milt's smelt was designed by Milt Jensen of Chico, California.

As we address the slip over technique with mylar tubing, it is impossible not to think of the incredible Zonker pattern. This pattern, designed by Dan Byford, holds its own with any of the top patterns known to fly fishing. The Zonker has produced big fish throughout the world in fresh, salt, warm, and cold waters. There have been many variations of the Zonker, but if it has a rabbit fur top strip and a mylar tubing body, it's a Zonker. The basic pattern is as follows and the variations are the same as hanging ornaments on the basic Christmas tree, such as painting eyes, shading the mylar with Pantone pens and even putting on gill plate sections. Use the color combinations best suited for imitating the small fish fry within the area you are fishing.

ZONKER — Plate #9 Fly #10

Hook: Tiemco 300 or Partridge D4A or Mustad 3665A
Body: Braided mylar tubing size 4-8 any color medium- large size back rabbit fur strip
Thread: 3/0

Step 1. Attach tape and cut on dotted line as shown.

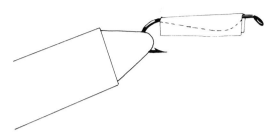

Step 2. Attach thread at the bend of the hook.

Step 3. Cut a piece of medium or large Mylar tubing, slightly longer than the shank of the hook. Pull out center cotton core.

Step 4. Slide the tubing over the hook shank and body, note that the frayed end of the tubing extends slightly beyond the tying thread.

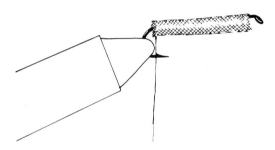

Step 5. Tie down the ends of the tubing, making a neat finished section. Whip finish and detach thread.

Step 6. Pull back the mylar tubing giving yourself at least 1 1/2 eye's width or hook shank to attach your thread to.

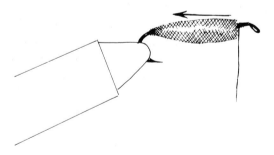

Step 7. Reattach tying thread and tie down the mylar tubing.

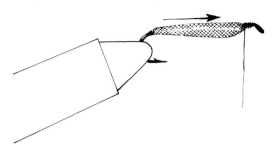

Step 8. Prepare a narrow strip of rabbit fur. The strip should be approximately ³/₁₆″ wide for sizes 2 through 6.

Note: When preparing the rabbit fur strip, the front end is trimmed to the hide. This bare section of hide will be where you tie down the front.

Step 9. Half-hitch the tying thread, and detach from the front of the fly.

Step 10. Reattach thread at the rear of the hook. Tie down rabbit strip as shown.

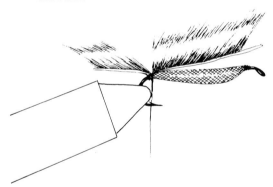

Step 11. Wet the rabbit fur and stroke back as shown, tie in using a soft loop. Tie down firmly with several wraps, whip finish and detach thread.

Step 12. Reattach tying thread on the front of the hook.

Step 13. Hold the front of the rabbit strip over the hook shank, tie down using a soft loop. Trim away excess hide.

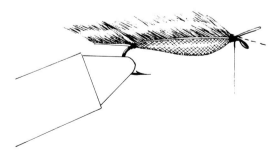

Step 14. Form a neat head and whip finish.

Step 15. Paint eyes as described in Applying Eyes to Flies (page 109).

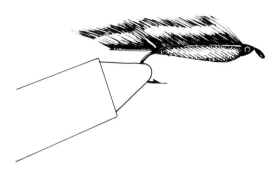

Note: This is the basic Zonker. However, in your travels you may find many variations and tying sequences. I'm sure Dan has a more refined version. One such variation is (Plate 9, fly #10)

MYLAR TUBING SALMON FLY

Hook: Partridge M-2
Underbody: Open cell foam
Overbody: Flourecent Mylar tubing (Everglow Tubing)
Tail: Mylar tubing
Wing: Fishair
Skirt: Mylar strands

Step 1. Attach thread and open cell foam.

Step 2. Form tapered foam underbody, no larger than the inner diameter of the mylar tubing.

Step 3. Leave thread hanging by the bend of the hook.

Step 4. Cut a piece of flourescent mylar tubing two times the length of the hook shank, and pull out cotton core.

Step 5. Fray one end of mylar tubing back approximately 1/2 the length of the hook shank.

Step 6. Slip tubing over the eye and foam body, until frayed ends hang back as tail.

Step 7. Tie down mylar tubing where fray and mesh join at the bend of the hook.

Step 8. Whip finish and detach thread.

Step 9. Fray back mylar until frayed section comes back to within one eye's width of the eye of the hook.

Step 10. Reattach tying thread to the front of the fly.

Step 11. Tie down mylar where the strands meet the mesh, one eye's width behind the eye.

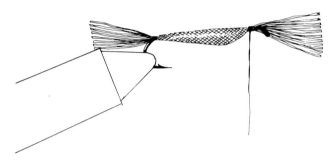

Step 12. Tie in wing.

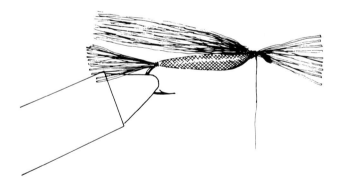

Step 13. Sweep back front mylar strands from head, whip finish and detach thread.

(Optional Step) Flourescent saddle hackle (same color as body) tied in at head area and swept back. (Shown in Plate 7, fly #4)

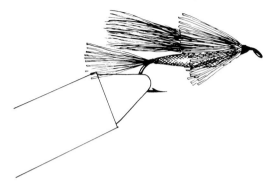

Note: Preferred colors for this pattern are orange, pink, and chartreuse.

Tips on Tying with Mylar Tubing

1. By fraying the end back approximately $1/2''$ and tying in at the end of the fray, you can create a very nice attracting skirt.

2. When coated with a clear lacquer or fingernail polish, the fish scale appearance becomes exaggerated.

3. By coating the entire body with a clear lacquer you will build in a longevity factor. The material will not fray as easily.

4. The tubing has a significant elongating factor. If the diameter is $1/4''$, you can stretch it over a $3/8''$ wide flat body.

SLIP OVER TECHNIQUE
WITH LARVA LACE BODY MATERIAL

The slip over method of tying with larva lace body material is one technique that makes this product so unique. The very same piece of tubing that a fly tyer just used to tie a size 4/6x long stone fly can be used to tie a size 18 chironomid. There are a few things to remember when tying with this technique and material.

A. Remember that the Larva Lace is soft, so when you rib with a fine thread the material will squeeze down and take the diameter of the hook. This is how you are able to obtain such a thin body appearance. By using Larva Lace translucent thread or a fine grade clear monofilament as thread, the body color will not be altered because the thread becomes invisible.

B. When the material is slipped over the shank remember that it will stretch forward when compressed to the hook. Because of this you will only cut approximately ³/₄ of the length that appears to be needed. It will take a couple of tries before you establish the length you need.

C. Hooks. The slip over technique lends itself to flys ranging from 16-20 in size. The hooks you choose will be determined by the design and wire size. Round eye and thin wire hooks are more desirable. If the hook eye is larger than the inner diameter of the tubing a drop of vegetable oil will do wonders as a lubricant. I keep a small finger nail polish jar filled with vegetable oil on my tying bench just for this technique. The small brush attached to the cap works perfectly as an applicator.

D. When starting the slip over make sure the material is cut on approximately a 45 degree angle. This allows you to enter the center hole of the material easier as well as giving you a tab to tie down to when starting your back wrap.

The following are some of the basic slip over patterns I use.

GREEN CADDIS LARVA — Plate #15, Fly #10
   Hook: Tiemco 2457-2487. Size 16-18
   Thread: Larva Lace translucent, ultra fine
   Body: Larva Lace chartreuse (#04) body material
   Collar: Black dyed coarse rabbit

Step 1. Attach thread by the bend of the hook.

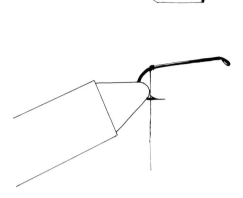

Step 2. Cut the end of the body material on a 45 degree angle. The body length should only be cut to 3/4 the length of the hook shank.

Step 3. Slip body material over the eye of the hook and tie down the abdomen.

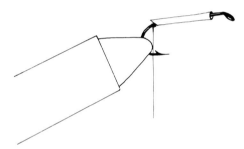

Step 4. Rib forward with close tight wraps.

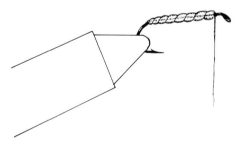

Step 5. Dub on a light amount of Black Coarse Rabbit for the collar and tie off. Use Dubbing Wax.

Tip: When ribbing forward you will find that you can taper the body by applying less pressure to the thread when nearing the front section of the fly body.

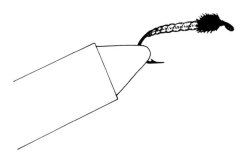

CAMERA'S MYSIS SHRIMP — Plate #15, Fly #6

   Hook: Tiemco TMC 200. Size 18-22
   Beard: Grizzly Hackle Fibers with two strands Pearl Crystal Hair.
   Thread: Larva Lace Translucent Clear, Ultra Fine
   Underbody: Pearl Crystal Fiber
   Overbody: Clear (#03) Larva Lace body material
   Legs: Grizzly Hackle Fibers

Step 1. Tie on hackle tips and wrap thread forward as illustrated.

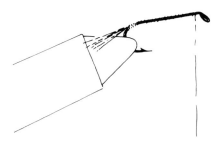

Step 2. Tie on crystal fiber, wrap thread to the rear of the hook.

Step 3. Wrap crystal fiber to the rear of the hook and cut off excess. Then build up head area with thread. (Head area is a to b.) Cut a piece of clear Larva Lace body material the length of the fly body then cut an angle on one end of the lace as illustrated.

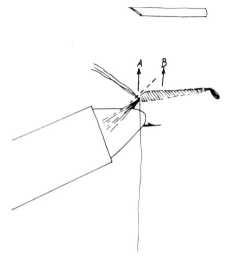

Step 4. Slide body material over the fly body.

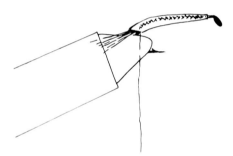

Step 5. With tying thread, make one turn in front and behind the head area (a-b), then rib using close wraps forward toward the hook eye. These wraps represent the segments in the shrimp body.

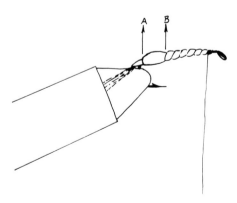

Step 6. Tie on throat hackle to represent legs. Apply eyes on head area of shrimp with black permanent marker. Whip finish and detach thread.

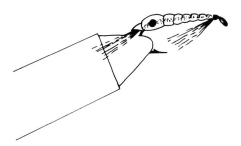

Tip: The eyes on this fly seem to be very important.

LARVA LACE MARCH BROWN — Plate #16, Fly #9
Hook: Mustad 3906B; Tiemco TMC-5262. Size 14-18
Tail: Brown Hackle Fiber
Thread: Larva Lace Clear Translucent, Ultra Fine
Body: Brown (#02) Larva Lace Body Material
Wing Case: Pheasant Tail
Thorax: Coarse Hare's Ear

Step 1. Tie in tail.

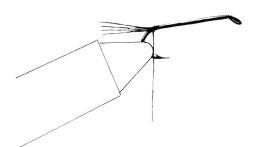

Step 2. Cut and slip over body material.

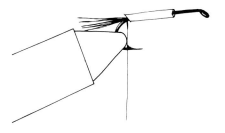

Step 3. Rib body with translucent thread.

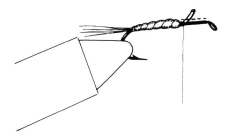

Step 4. Tie in wing case.

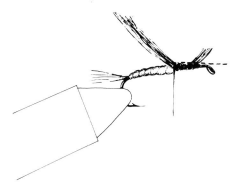

Step 5. Dub Thorax.

Step 6. Pull over wing case and tie off.

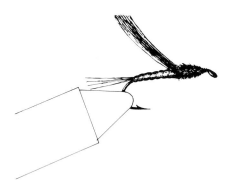

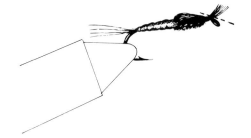

Step 7. Pull out thorax with dubbing brush.

BLOOD WORM — Plate #13, Fly #8

Hook: Tiemco T400. Size 12-14
Thread: 8/0 Red Uni-Thread
Body: Orange (#10) Larva Lace Body Material

Step 1. Attach thread at bend of the hook.

Step 2. Cut larva lace to size.

Step 3. Apply vegetable oil to hook shank.

Step 4. Slip over larva lace.

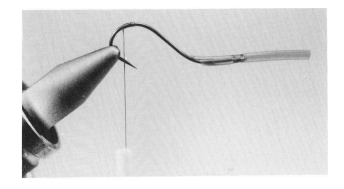

Tip-Make sure you are pushing in the same plane as the hook.

Step 5. Tie in abdomen as you would when tying the head. Then proceed toward the front with close tight segmentations.

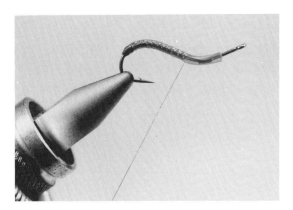

Step 6. Tie off the head and put a light coat of vinyl cement on the entire fly. The vinyl cement will help prevent the ribbed thread from fraying.

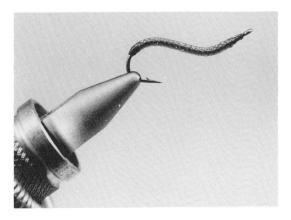

HALF HITCH WEAVE

The half hitch weave is one of the most exciting and fun to use when tying with the many new materials available today. This technique of tying lends itself to an enormous variety of patterns proven to be productive in cold, warm, and salt water.

While conducting a fly tying clinic at Larry Walkers' Fishing Hole in Denver, Colorado, I was tying a conventional weave pattern when Doyle Walt asked me how Larva Lace worked with the half-hitch methods. I told him I was unfamiliar with that technique but if he would sit down and tie it we would both know. As Doyle started his stone fly body with two different colors of lace it was evident that we were in for a lot of fun. The eyes around the table started to widen at the ease and results of a beautiful looking stone fly body. Here was a weave technique that you could teach to a 5 year old student and have him or her tying within 10 minutes.

While Doyle was captivating my clinic I was standing there just thinking of all the neat things that I was going to do with this. In the past, this technique of weaving was done with flosses and other softer materials which lent themselves more to what I call the conventional weave method. With the smooth round surface of vinyl tubular materials, this technique of fly tying has been resurrected. This method of weave can also be used with many other combinations of new synthetic materials. The results will be exciting.

The general procedures for tying the Half Hitch Weave are photographically illustrated below in the River Witch pattern.

The River Witch is very similar to the famed Bitch Creek except it has a large head and swept back hackle and no rubber legs; additionally, Marabou is substituted for the tail.

RIVER WITCH — Plate # 10, Fly # 6

Materials:
Hook: Mustad 79580. Size 4-10
Tail: Marabou
Underbody cover: Pearl Mylar over open cell foam
Body: Larva Lace Body Material
Head: Black Chenille
Hackle: Black Spey (larger hackles from the neck)

Step 1. Tie in marabou tail. (heavy)

Step 2. Tie in body material

    A. The color desired for the back should be tied on the side of the hook away from you.

    B. The color desired for the belly should be tied on the side of the hook closest to you.

Step 3. Tie in a strip of pearl mylar. This is used to overwrap our underbody of foam. When this fly is completed the Mylar will sparkle between the joints of the half-hitch weave.

Step 4. Tie in a strip of open cell foam, leaving foam and tinsel hanging off the back.

Step 5. Form a tapered body with open cell foam.

Step 6. Overwrap foam with flat Mylar strip.

Step 7. Tie off thread, remove it from the fly and face the vise and fly toward you.

Step 8. Knot the Larva Lace as illustrated. Always bring the light piece over the top of the dark. Now separate and slip the dark piece over the shank of the hook, then slide both pieces to the rear. Place both pieces of Larva Lace between thumb and forefinger of each hand holding as close as possible to the hook and pull the knot tight.

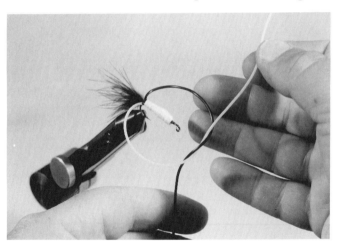 

When pulling the knot tight make sure that you pull directly out from the side, not up or down.

Step 9. Continue these knots until you have come up ³/₄ of the shank of the hook.

Step 10.
   A. Reattach tying thread
   B. Tie down larva lace and cut off surplus.

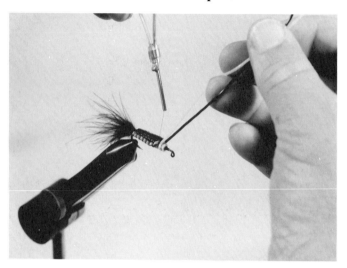

Step 11. Tie in spey hackle-tip first. When tying in hackle come back onto weave area by at least two knots.

Step 12. Tie in chenille; strip end of chenille and come back at least two knots into the weave.

Step 13. Wrap chenille to form head. Head should be ¹/₃ the length of the body.

Step 14.
   A. Fold spey hackle keeping shiny side out.
   B. Palmer Hackle through the head of River Witch
   C. Tie off

Tied smaller than size 12, this fly is still productive. It does become a lot more difficult to tie. Because of its difficulty, the name changes to Son of a Witch.

The River Witch has proven itself in most all types of waters and when fished at all depths.

MINI CRAWDAD — Plate #11, Fly #4

Hook: Mustad 37160. Size 4-8
Thread: Brown
Feelers: Hackle Fiber
Claws: Ring Neck Pheasant Booster Back Feathers
Eyes: Burnt 20 lb. Mono
Tail: Ringneck Pheasant Hen Back Feather
Underbody: Open Cell Foam Strip
Body: Reddish Brown (#11) Larva Lace Body Material
Beard: Mallard Flank Feather Fibers

Step 1. Tie in Beard

Step 2. Tie in larva lace body material as shown for half-hitch weave. Half-hitch the thread and separate from fly.

Step 3. Make one half-hitch knot and tie thread back on to the fly.

Step 4. Prepare pre-made claws as follows:

    A. Pluck two ring neck pheasant rooster breast feathers.
    B. Strip off the web.
    C. Cut the stem of the feather approx $3/8$ of an inch down from the top —do not cut the feather, cut only the stem.
    D. When stem is cut, lacquer both sides of feather and your claw is made.

Step 5. Tie one claw on each side of the fly. Detach thread

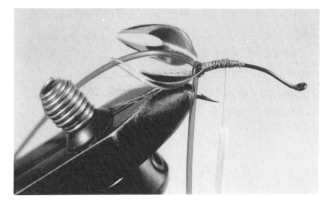

Step 6. Tie one more half-hitch knot and reattach the tying thread.

Step 7. Install feelers

Step 8. Install burnt mono eyes

Step 9. Tie on white open cell foam

Step 10. Form underbody with foam

When forming underbody, taper the body so that the foam ends approximately ¼ the shank length from the eye.

Step 11. Remove thread from the fly

Step 12. Proceed in tying half-hitch knots along the body until you have gone at least one knot past the foam.

Step 13. Reattach tying thread to the fly and tie off the larva lace.

Step 14. Prepare pre-made tail

Instructions for pre-made tail:

    A. Pluck small feather from the back section of a ring neck pheasant hen cape.
    B. Snip off web.
    C. Cut the stem the same as you did with the claw.
    D. Strip the feather down to make it proportionally correct.
    E. Lacquer both sides.

Step 15. Tie on pre-made tail

P.C. SMELT — Plate #6, Fly #3

Materials:

Hook: Mustad 79580. Size 2-4

Underbody: Open Cell Foam with Pearl Mylar Tinsel Wrapped Over.

Overbody: Clear (#03) Larva Lace Body Material, half-hitch weave over full length of body

Tail: White Marabou

Thread: Larva Lace Translucent – Fine

The P.C. Smelt is a streamer with a marabou tail and half-hitch woven body. This fly is nothing more than an exercise in tying the over hand knot. The thing that makes it unique is that the over hand is tied vertically instead of horizontally, thus giving the appearance of a scaled fish body. Prism tape eyes are glued on and lacquered over.

This pattern will imitate almost any fry simply by coloring the underbody foam with pantone pens before the clear half-hitch technique is completed.

Catalpa Worm

Being from the Northern regions of the United States, I had never seen or heard of a Catalpa Worm. As I started traveling and becoming more involved with fisherman throughout the nation, I repeatedly heard of a Catalpa Worm. To this day, I still have not seen one, but as described to me by many, it is a rather chunky tri-colored caterpillar. Technically, it is the larvae of the catalpa sphinx moth. It falls from the branches of the Catalpa tree. This little fellow makes his appearance in the spring and entices fish within his region until late June.

I've been told that my woven pattern looks very similar to the real thing, but most importantly, it works well on bass, crappie and blue gill. This same pattern is tied on a black jig head hook and works equally well with a spinning rig.

CATALPA WORM — Plate #10, Fly #7

Materials:
Hook: Mustad 37160. Size 6-10
Thread: Black 6/0 Uni-Thread
Underbody: Open Cell Foam
Body: Black (#01) and Chartreuse (#4) Larva Lace Body Material tied with the Half Hitch Weave Technique. Black Back/ Chartreuse belly.
Tail: Black Hackle Fibers
Legs: Black Saddle Hackle Tied as a Throat
Collar: Black Rabbit Dubbing

Step 1. Tie in small rabbit hair dubbed abdomen.

Step 2. Tie in two hackle fibers for the tail section.

Step 3. Tie in black Larva Lace body material on the back side of the hook.

Step 4. Tie in chartreuse Larva Lace body material on the front side of the hook.

Step 5. Tie in a strip of open cell foam.

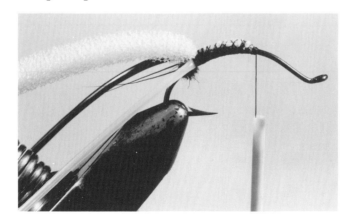

Step 6. Wrap open cell foam forward forming a firm underbody and tie off.

Step 7. Detach tying thread.

Step 8. Tie half hitch weave the full length of the body leaving two eye widths for room to tie off.

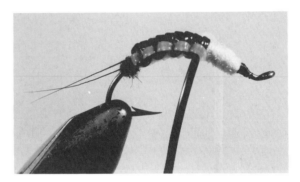

Step 9. Reattach tying thread and tie off the Larva Lace body material.

Step 10. Attach and wrap black saddle hackle tying it back with a swept back appearance.

Step 11. Trim off hackle on the top of the fly leaving only the bottom to look like legs.

Step 12. Dub on a light collar of black rabbit and whip finish.

Step 13. Detach thread and head cement tie off area.

THE CONVENTIONAL WEAVE

The conventional weave is a technique that is described in George F. Grant's book *The Master Fly Weaver*, when discussing his "Mossback" style of Nymph body. I call this the conventional weave, because it seems that most every time I see weave demonstrations the technique seems to be that of Grant's "Mossback."

Without question, I feel that this technique of weaving is the most accepted and versatile in today's flytyer's bag of tricks. Many of our great Western U.S. tyers capitalized on this technique when bringing us such patterns as the Bitch Creek, George Anderson's Stone Fly Nymph, and the ever famous Hank Robert's Woven Flys. One of the reasons for its popularity is its compatibility with dissimilar materials. What I mean by that, is you can weave vinyl tubing with angora or chenille, with floss or most any other combination to come up with some incredible effects. The following pattern will demonstrate what I call the conventional weave.

BITCH CREEK — Plate #10, Fly #1

Materials:
Hook: Mustad 79580 or Dai-Riki 700. Size 6-12
Tail: White elastic
Back: Black Chenille
Belly: Yellow Chenille
Thorax: Black Chenille
Hackle: Brown
Antennae: White elastic
Underbody: Open Cell Foam

Step 1. Tie in elastic tail.

Step 2. Tie black chenille onto the opposite side of the hook.

Step 3. Tie the yellow chenille onto the hook on the side closest to you.

Step 4. Tie in a piece of open cell foam and form a tapered body. Whip finish and separate the thread from the fly.

Step 5. With the vise pointing to your right, take the black chenille in your right hand and make one complete reverse wrap around the base of the hook.

Step 6. With the right hand bring the black chenille across the back of the fly and hook it with the yellow by bringing the yellow chenille around the black from back to front. When the two colors of chenille are hooked, bring the black back across the back of the fly and the yellow under the belly of the fly.

Step 7. When the two chenille pieces meet on the far side of the fly, repeat the same procedure by bringing the yellow chenille around the black and under the belly and the black across the back of the fly.

Step 8. Re-attach the tying thread, but don't let go of the two pieces of chenille.

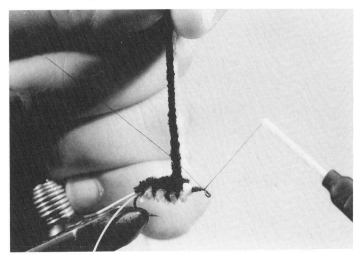

Step 9. Tie down the chenille weave so the weave won't unravel. Cut off only the yellow piece.

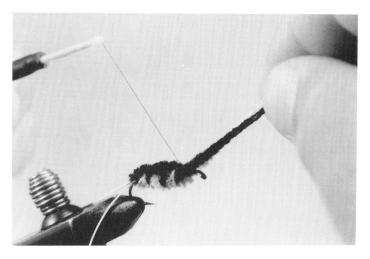

Step 10. Attach elastic antennas, brown hackle and open cell foam.

Step 11. Form small underbody for the thorax.

Step 12. Wrap thorax with black chenille.

Step 13. Palmer long soft saddle hackle the length of the thorax.

Step 14. Whip finish and separate the thread.

Tips: When fishing this nymph in slow water, I will leave the antennas and tail long (the length of the body).When fishing in faster water I like them about half the length of the body.

CONVENTIONAL WRAP METHOD USING LARVA LACE BODY MATERIAL

Conventional Wrap when Using an Underbody

When tying the conventional wrap method, there are a couple things you need to think about before starting. Depending upon the appearance you are looking for, consider minimal build up at the tie in area and overall appearance having a large or small segmented look.

To insure minimal build up when using an underbody, you need to cut the end of the tubular body material so that it is pointed on the end. Tie in one half of the point to the bend of the hook. When you start to wrap, the material will stretch. Make one complete wrap around the hook itself, then start to wrap forward, letting each wrap lay in evenly along side of the previous wrap. The easiest way that I have found to make these wraps even is to slightly over wrap so that it lies on the previous turn, then slide off nice and close to the previous turn. Once you start tying this way, it will look like your hand is not only going around the hook, but also moving slightly back and forth. Additionally, using this technique will insure that portions of your underbody will not pop through.

Conventional Wrap when Used Without an Underbody

There are many patterns that call for a silver, gold or pearl mylar wrap over the shank of the hook for the finished body. These patterns are mostly for streamers and when the fish see them, they hit hard. You will find that by using a wrap of clear body material over the mylar, you will build in a very high durability factor. These flies will last you a great deal longer, plus, it will enhance their appearance as well.

Tie on your choice of clear body material the full length of the hook, leaving only the width of the hook's eye as a gap from the front. As you tie down your material, take advantage of its elasticity and stretch it along the back of the hook. The thread will compress it to the shank as you wrap, so you need not worry about build up. Place the mylar over the top of the clear material and tie it down the same way – bringing your tying thread forward. Wrap your mylar using the conventional wrap and tying off at the front, then follow with the conventional wrap with clear body material over the mylar.

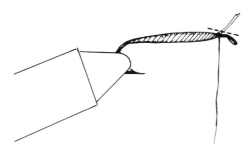

Completed durable streamer body. Mylar wrap first, then follow with clear body material

Underbodies for the Conventional Wrap

There have been all kinds of underbodies used, but very few lend themselves to flytying like open cell foam. For years tyers have purchased it under the names of Art Foam, Hobby Foam, and even foam sheet fabric softeners have been used after mom finished with her laundry. Most of those days are behind us now because there are a number of companies putting out open cell foam just for the fly tyer. See the section on foam tying techniques for a more complete discussion of foam.

THE LEG WEAVE

The weave technique I call the Leg Weave is similar to the technique patented by Franz B. Potts (March 6, 1934; patent #1949582). The difference between the two is that Mr. Potts brought both materials being woven over the shank of the hook during each weave segment. With the leg weave I only bring the material used for the body over the hook. The leg material wrapped around the body only, not the hook shank. This technique is explained in the photo sequence of the Larva Lace shrimp. (See cover photo.) When originated, Potts used his weave when tying the famed Sandy Mite. The leg material was three strands of unwaxed burnt orange tying thread or mono cord size A. The body was made of Sandy Ox hair. When woven the orange thread gave a woven rib line along the belly. If the ox hair was to break after catching a few fish, the rib would stay intact because of being wrapped around the hook. With today's tough synthetics used for body material, we can take a few short cuts and still have a very durable fly. In reducing this technique to its simplest form, it is the same as tying only one side of the conventional weave. The following pattern will demonstrate the leg weave.

LACE SHRIMP – Reference Cover Photo

This shrimp pattern is one of the most unique I've seen, and its productivity is equally high. I first came across this crustacean at the 1988 Denver Sportsman's Exposition. It was being tied by its originator, Mike Tucker of Lakewood, Colorado. When examining this pattern, I was intrigued with the legs as well as its shape. This fly is fished as a scud or shrimp that has been washed off a weed bed. A deep natural drift seems to be most effective.

LACE SHRIMP — Plate #12, Flys # 11 & 12
Materials:
Hook: Mustad 37160 or Eagle Claw 141. Size 14-16
Beard: Mallard Flank Feather
Body: Larva Lace Body Material
Thread: Larva Lace translucent (clear)
Legs: Ostrich Herl
Colors: Clear, with Pearl Crystal insert; Olive; Larva Lace shrimp color; Orange; grey

Step 1. Insert a 4″ piece of Crystal Hair in a piece of Larva Lace Body Material. (See pg. 78, How to insert Crystal Fibers into Hollow Body Material.)

Step 2. Tie in beard by the bend of the hook.

Step 3. Tie in a small piece of Larva Lace to the top part of the hump section of the hook. Clip off the excess, leaving a built up hump area.

Step 4. Cut a sharp angle on another small piece of Larva Lace and repeat step 3., except for cutting off the excess. (Leave the body material attached.)

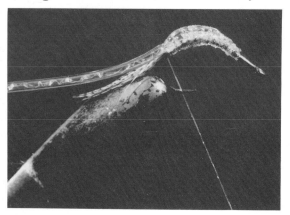

Step 5. Attach ostrich herl, keeping the herl directly on the bottom of the fly. Bring the thread forward to the eye of the hook and give it a half hitch. It is best at this point to place the thread and bobbin 5 or 6 inches off to your right, so it won't interfere with the next step.

Step 6. Wrap Larva Lace around the shrimp two times, hold the lace toward yourself when finished.

Step 7. Wrap ostrich herl around the Larva Lace, then wrap the lace around the hook. Continue this procedure down the hook shank, wrap herl around Lace, wrap lace around hook.

Step 8. Continue until you have gone approximately ³/₄ of the way down the hook shank, then cut and separate the ostrich from the fly.

Step 9. Finish wrapping the body material to within one eye's width of the hook eye. Tie off and separate thread from the fly.

Step 10. Using your fingernail, slide the legs back to the bottom of the fly by lightly slipping the ostrich through the wraps.

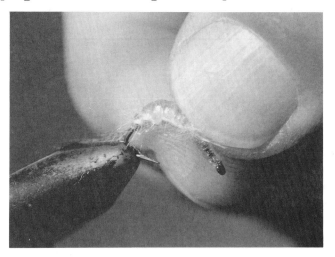

Step 11. While the fly is still in the vise, make small black eyes with a high quality permanent marker.

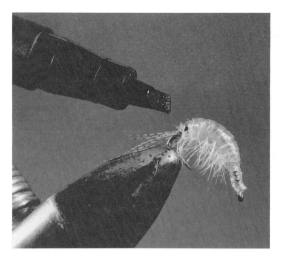

Tip: If you find that you have a few extra herl fibers along the back, all you need to do is protect the legs and beard with your fingers and singe the unwanted fiber off with a match.

Note: The shrimp on the cover does not have crystal fiber through the Lace.

THE INTERNAL
RIBBING EFFECT TECHNIQUE

When tying the conventional wrap we find many patterns calling for a very fine ribbing. By using the internal ribbing technique, we can obtain a large variety of effects. The internal ribbing technique is nothing more than inserting another material through the center of a hollow translucent body material before starting a conventional wrap. An item that you may find effective is dark color 8 to 10 lb. monofilament fish line. When inserted into orange body material, it creates a dark exoskeleton effect on the body. With all of the new synthetics and hair fibers available, the effects made possible are literally endless. One of my favorites is a Crazy Charlie bone fish fly tied with shrimp color Larva Lace body material, with orange crystal flash inserted through the tubing.

(Ref. Tying Techniques with Crystal Fibers, page 77.)

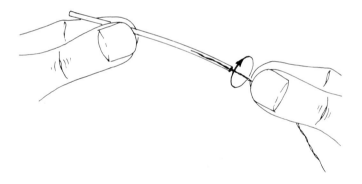

COLOR BLENDING WITH TRANSLUCENT MATERIALS

The best way to get the most out of translucent materials is to know and remember the different effects of color blending. I have found that one of the easiest ways of learning color effect is to take a #8 shank hook (Mustad 94720) in about a size 4 and wrap a different color on it every $3/16$ of and inch. Then, wrap a single piece of colored translucent body material over the entire length of the shank, exposing all the different shades that can be obtained with that color of translucent material. The color and shade combinations are virtually endless.

On some of my favorite patterns I will overwrap a different color of body material just to tone down a certain underbody color, while still retaining the full translucent effect. When tying these patterns you will find that when using nylon translucent thread you will not affect the color of the body material.

With color effects, experimentation and experience are the keys, so don't be afraid to play with it so that you can find the color or shade that you are looking for.

THE SPARKLE DUNK TECHNIQUE

I know that if people don't read any other part of this book, they will most likely turn to this technique just to see what this is all about. The Sparkle Dunk technique may sound pretty weird, but it makes the prettiest and most uniform body you could want. I use this technique on Crazy Charlies and Streamer Bodies when trying to obtain an internal sparkle effect. This is certainly not a technique that you would use for a production fly but it sure is fun if you care about a good looking finished product.

SPARKLE DUNK CRAZY CHARLIE — Reference Plate #8, Fly #4

Materials:

Hook: Mustad 34007-Skinless. Size 2-8

Underbody: Open Cell Foam (Glitter Pen used over Foam, Ultra Fine Glitter-Used over Glitter Pen)

Body: Clear Larva Lace Body Material

Tail: White Calf Tail

Wing: White Calf Tail with 2 thru 4 strands of pearl crystal hair.

Thread: Clear Larva Lace translucent

Eye: Medium Size silver bead chain

Tips.

1. Glitter pens can be found at most any craft store. This is a small fine nose plastic bottle with glitter that the kids use to write on T-Shirts with. This product comes in many colors and will add a great deal of experimental time to your fly tying.

2. Ultra Fine Glitter will most likely be found in the same section as the bottles. This material is dry and can be used simply by removing the lid and dunking in the fly. The material will stick to the wet surface of the glitter pen.

3. When making this fly I normally tie a couple of dozen and let them all dry together.

Tying Steps for the Sparkle Dunk Crazy Charlie

Step 1. Tie in Calf Tail for the Tail.

Step 2. Tie on a 4″ piece of clear Larva Lace body material.

Step 3. Tie in a strip of open cell foam. Then form a tapered body.

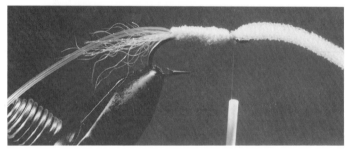

Step 4. Apply Pearl Glitter Pen to the foam body

Note: This will look like Elmers Glue with tiny pieces of glitter in it.

Step 5. Spread this material evenly around the entire foam body.

Step 6. Dunk the entire fly in a jar of ultra fine glitter.

Remove the fly and shake lightly. Stick the fly on your rotary drying rack and let cure. (see Plate 3, Item 4)

Step 7. Place body on drying rotary.

Step 8. After body is fully cured wrap clear larva lace body material over the glitter body. Tie off.

Step 9. Attach bead chain eyes.

Step 10. Turn fly over and attach white calf tail wings. Inter mix 2-4 strands of pearl crystal hair in with the calf tail.

Step 11. Complete the head with translucent thread and tie off.

Step 12. Secure the fly with head cement.

LIQUID FILLED FLIES

After introducing Larva Lace body material in 1985 it didn't take long for people to start putting all types of substances into the center hole to obtain a certain effect. One of my favorites is Crystal Hair because of its attracting characteristics, however, in the past few years there have been many people toying with the liquid filling of Larva Lace while tying their flies. This group of tyers does not seem to be growing too fast and may be because this technique of tying requires a little more than it's worth. The main ingredient used for liquid filled flys is vegetable oil. The claims are that by using oil filled materials you could enhance translucency and obtain a natural buoyancy. That could be true if you were able to fit enough vegetable oil in the tube. However, through many self tests, the tiny amount that fits inside the tying material appears to have no measurable effect on buoyancy.

Some of the positive factors I have found have been color shading and scenting.

The most popular liquids used for filling are:

A. Vegetable Oil
B. Food Color and Water
C. Shrimp or Fish Oil

Methods of Applying Liquid to Hollow Body Material

Technique A

1. Take a 24″ piece of larva lace body material and put one end in a cup of vegetable oil.

2. Put the other end in your mouth and suck. Keep eye on the liquid and stop just before it enters your mouth. Take the lace out of your mouth and tie an overhand knot, leaving other end in liquid. Then take out the other end and tie another overhand knot on it.

3. Wipe the ends dry and tie a series of two overhand knots every six inches. Make sure these knots are tied very tight.

4. Cut the lace between the two knots and you will end up with four strands ready to tie with.

Technique B

1. Take a six inch piece of lace and tie an overhand knot in one end.

2. Fill end of the lace by using a fine, short hypodermic needle and tie an overhand knot in the other end.

Because this technique is new to fly tying, only time will tell if it will hold its own or is just a passing interest. Whatever it may be, I encourage you to add it to your experimental list of tying techniques.

Tips for Tying Liquid Filled Flies —

1. Keep feathers or other tying materials from oil filling area.

2. Add a spittoon to your fly tying equipment list.

TYING TECHNIQUES WITH CRYSTAL FIBERS

This type of material has made a major impact on the fly tying industry. The extensive variety of combinations that the tyer can apply is creating a whole new world of tying. As mentioned in the introduction, flys are tied as duplicators, simulators or attractors. When using the Crystal Fibers we are combining the simulators with the attractors. By taking many of our old proven patterns and adding a sparse amount of glitter we have found, in many cases, improved performance and productivity. These flies may be used more on overcast days, in slightly off-colored water, or even when fished deep. However, in all three instances I have found higher performance with certain patterns when these fibers were introduced.

How about the attractors? Whoa! In Alaska, the salmon and steelhead see this as we saw the transition from the flintlock to the breach-loading firearm. They knew they were in trouble. The following tips will explain a few ways to use these fibers when fly tying.

1. When applying to conventional patterns, use sparsely. Two or three small pieces will be enough in many cases.

2. When mixing in with tail or wing material, blend it in so that the flashy fibers are in the center rather than the top or side. First wing fibers, then crystal fibers, then more wing fibers.

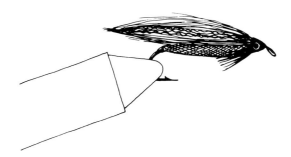

3. By inserting crystal fibers into Larva Lace body material a glitter can be created from within the fly body. To create an exoskeleton effect, use the same procedure as described for Internal Ribbing Technique. (see Internal Ribbing page 67.)

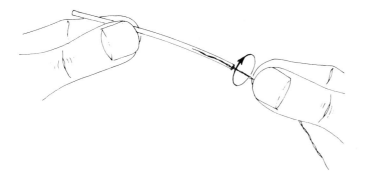

How to Insert Crystal Fibers into Hollow Body Material

1. Determine the length of the hollow body material you will need to tie your chosen pattern.

2. Cut body material on sharp angle — this creates a larger hole opening.

3. Cut a piece of crystal flash approximately 1″ longer than the body material.

4. Grip tubing between thumb and forefinger of right hand. Get a grip near the end of the material.

5. When using Larva Lace, lay it on a flat surface with approximately ½″ hanging over the edge of the surface. Insure the tubing is straight.

6. Hold Crystal Fiber in left hand between thumb and forefinger and insert into center of the body material. As you are pushing the fiber in, rotate the fiber between your fingers. You will see the fiber going in like a drill. Make sure that you keep the body material on a flat surface and as straight as possible. For most patterns, five inches will be enough.

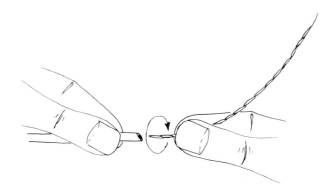

For those rare occasions when you need a longer piece, use the following procedure:

a) Go to your local hobby crafts store and purchase a .015 diameter piece of piano wire. This will come in approximately 3 inch lengths.

b) Cut a piece of Larva Lace body material approximately 2″ shorter than the length of material you want to thread through it.

c) Insert the piano wire through the body material, leaving approximately 2″ of the wire sticking out.

d) Wrap the insert material around the wire about 10 turns.

e) Keeping the wrapped material tight, place a drop of quick drying head cement on the turns and hold until it drys.

f) Place a few drops of vegetable oil on the wire and pull the material through.

Tying in Crystal Fibers

These fibers are very slick and tend to pull out if not locked in. To lock in the crystal fibers you must fold the fiber back over itself, then tie down in the folded area.

Crystal Fibers can also be used to conventionally wrap on hook shanks, which are then overwrapped with clear body material for an additional protection.

Crystal Fibers can also be used as wing case on tiny midge nymphs.

Flash Back Nymph

Many tiny Midge Nymph bodies are wrapped with Crystal Fiber. (Size 18-24) Be sure to put a protective coating of head cement or translucent thread over the fibers to gain some longevity.

Flash Back Nymph

The Flash Back is an excellent example of how synthetics are giving some older patterns a face lift. In most cases this technique is applied to the May Fly Nymph. Ranging from the March Brown, the Pheasant Tail, Ginger Quill and the many others, what identifies them as a flashback is the use of a Silver or Pearl Mylar wing case in place of the original pattern's wing case. Some people prefer Crystal Hair for these.

Most all of these patterns have already proven themselves, so what we are doing is offering a little more attracting capability to the fly. There are times, when in faster water or when the fly is just on the edge of the fish's vision window, the little extra reflecting action can make the difference of a pick-up or nothing.

I'm not sure who started the Flash Back, but whoever it was, I commend them for another innovative technique of tying with synthetics. I've heard rumors that it was started in the U.K., others say it was New Zealand. I've seen it tied in Colorado since the early 1980's. Whatever its origin, I still suggest you give it a try.

Some Popular Flash Back Patterns

PHEASANT TAIL FLASH BACK — (Plate #16, Fly #7)
Materials:
Hook: Tiemco 3769; Mustad 3906 or 3906B. Size 10-18
Tail: Pheasant Tail
Body: Pheasant Tail
Wing Case: Pearl Crystal Hair
Thorax: Peacock Herl

GOLD RIBBED HARE'S EAR FLASH BACK — Plate #16, Fly #7
Materials:
Hook: Tiemco 3760; Mustad 3906 or 3906B. Size 10-18
Tail: Black Stiff Hackle Fibers
Rib: Fine Copper Wire
Body: Wrapped Closed Cell Foam, Black
Wing Case: Pearl Crystal Hair
Thorax: Dubbed Black Coarse Rabbit

BIOT FLASH BACK
Materials:
Hook: Tiemco 100; Mustad 94840. Size 16-24
Tail: Hackle Fibers
Body: Black Biot, Wrapped
Wing Case: Pearl Crystal Hair
Thorax: Black Rabbit or Seal X

Black & Twinkle Spider (British Pattern)

The Black & Twinkle is a synthetic version of the well known black & peacock spider. The substitution of Twinkle has resulted in many larger than average fish being caught on this fly. It has been particularly effective for catching rainbow trout and grayling. Best results are achieved when fished slow and deep.

BLACK AND TWINKLE SPIDER (British Pattern)

Materials:
Hook: Partridge Captain Hamilton L2A. Size 10-14
Thread: Black Supergrip
Underbody: LED, flat lead (optional)
Body: Black Lureflash Twinkle
Hackle: Black Hen

Step 1. Add weight to the hook by adding a few turns of flat lead (LED). Tie on tying thread.

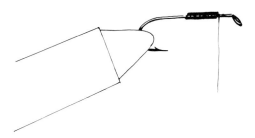

Step 2. Wrap thread to rear of hook and tie in 3 or 4 strands of black Lureflash Twinkle. Build a tapered body with thread and black Lureflash.

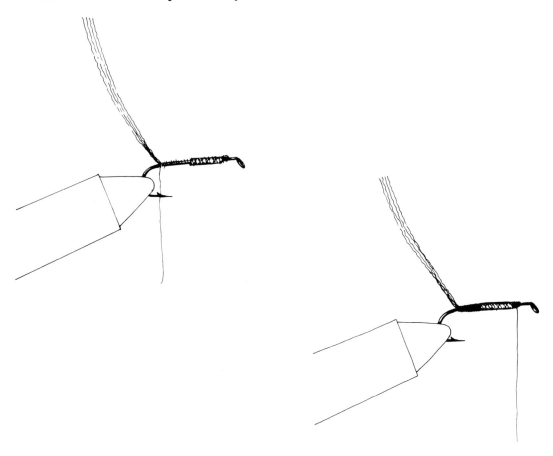

Step 3. Tie in a soft hen hackle and wind 3 or 4 turns. Tie off.

Step 4. Build up the head with thread, whip finish and head cement.

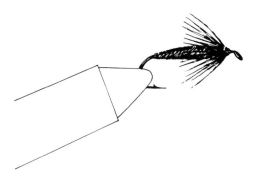

Mosaic Viva (British Pattern)

The Mosaic Viva was developed by Stephen Gross, of Yorkshire, England. Its success at attracting trout has been truly remarkable. It can be tied on hooks size 8 to 14 with equal effect and used as a point fly with droppers or as a single fly on a long leader. This fly is best fished on a floating line with a very slow rate of retrieve. Be prepared for very gentle takes indicated by the slightest movement of the leader.

THE MOSAIC VIVA

Materials:
Hook: Partridge L/S 8 D4A Streamer
Thread: Black Supergrip
Tail: Fluorescent Lime Green Antron Body Wool
Rib: 6 strands Blue Lureflash Mobile
Body: Black Chenille
Wing: Mosaic Lureflash Mobile

Step 1. Wrap the hook with thread to the bend.

Step 2. Tie in fluorescent Lime Green Antron to form tail.

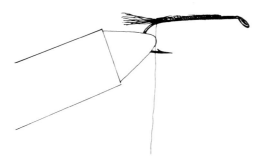

Step 3. Tie in black chenille and six strands of blue Lureflash at the bend of the hook. Wrap thread to the hook eye.

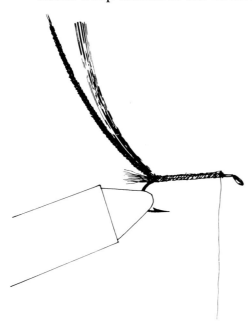

Step 4. Wind chenille up to the eye of the hook. Tie off and detach the chenille, leave thread hanging.

Step 5. Twist strands of Lureflash together to form a round rope and rib along
body.

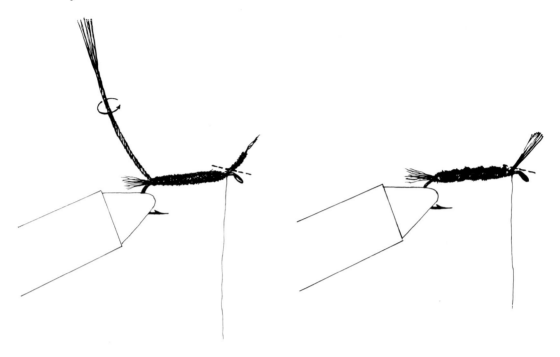

Step 6. Tie in Mosaic Lureflash to form wing.

Step 8. Build head, whip finish and head cement.

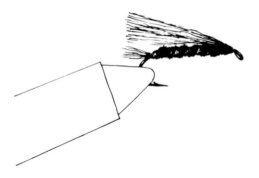

Floating Fritz and Frondz Flies (British Pattern)

This pattern can be tied with either Fritz or Frondz as the body material. It has
proven to be very effective as a floating fry pattern in all colors and in various
conditions. White has been demonstrated to be particularly effective when
trout are fry feeding.

During the rest of the season, when the water is cold and the fish are slow and deep, the flies are best fished on a sinking line with a very short leader above the weeds. Retrieve with a slow sink and draw method. Be prepared for gentle takes as the fly rises in the water after each draw of the line.

FRITZ AND FRONDZ FLIES

Hook: Partridge GRS 4A. Sizes 8-12
Back: Closed Cell Foam
Tail: Marabou to match back
Body: Lureflash Fritz or Frondz or Crystal Chenille to match back
Thread: Fluorescent color to match other materials

Step 1. Attach thread and tie down marabou tail.

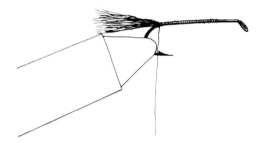

Step 2. Tie down Fritz, Frondz or chenille for body and wrap thread forward.

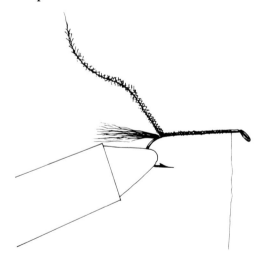

Step 3. Wrap on body material, taking care to sweep fibers toward the back of the hook after each wrap.

Step 4. Cut a strip of closed cell foam as illustrated and tie down behind the hook eye. Whip finish and detach tying thread.

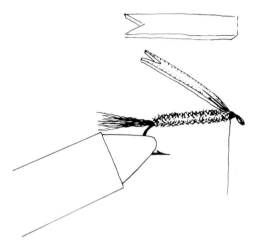

Step 5. Reattach tying thread at point "A" and tie down the foam at bend of hook.

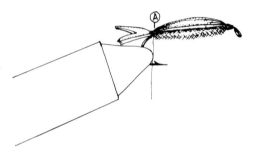

Step 6. Trim foam to length and cut vee in tail. Apply head cement to tie down areas. Be careful not to allow head cement to mix with foam — the foam might dissolve.

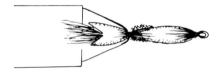

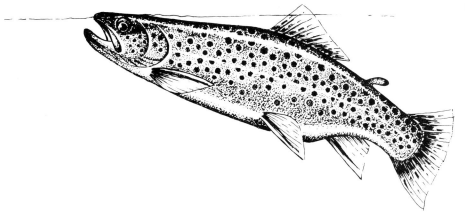

FOAM TYING TECHNIQUES

Foam is increasing in popularity as a fly tying material. We have all seen many patterns calling for foam, usually for dry flys or emergers. Most tyers believe that because it is foam, it must float. Well, that isn't always true.

The two kinds of foam most commonly used for fly tying are open cell and closed cell. Entire volumes could be written on the chemistry involved in manufacturing these foams, however, either kind will float or sink depending on the technique used in tying.

The most commonly used closed cell foam is called Evazote, in the fly tackle industry it is usually called "dry fly foam." This foam has a cell structure which captures tiny pockets of air, thereby offering a high buoyancy factor. It is generally used for dry flies, but if wrapped tight, or in the area of tie down, there will be a decrease in floatation. The explanation for this is simple, when you compress the foam, air is forced out of the pockets and the area of dispersion is reduced.

Open cell foam has a physical structure much like that of a common sponge. With that comparison it should be apparent why this is the foam preferred when tying wet flies. In addition, it is good for a lot more than just soaking up water. Open cell foam will also soak up a high grade floatant, and, because of the many tiny canals and interwoven channels it takes quite a while for the floatant to dissipate. Many dry fly patterns can be tied with open cell foam, as long as the foam is dressed properly.

Another unique feature of foam as tying material is its ability to lie flat and firm when building and tapering underbodies. In fact, I have become so dependent on it that I now have a hard time tying without it.

Patterns Which Feature Closed Cell Foam:

BLACK ANT — Plate #14, Fly #18

Originated by Eddie Chiles
Materials:
Hook: TMC 101. Size 16-20
Body: Black Closed Cell Foam
Thread: 8/0 Black Uni-Thread
Hackle: Black

Step 1. Attach thin strip of black closed cell foam (evazote) half way back towards the bend of the hook.

Step 2. Make 3 to 4 wraps toward the bend of the hook, then follow back with tying thread to the bend tying down the last wrap.

Step 3. Bring thread forward to mid-section then fold over the foam creating a hump.

Step 4. Tie off the hump and wrap 2 to 3 turns in the front section, creating the underbody for the next hump.

Step 5. Bring foam forward making the forward hump and tie off at the hook eye. Detach excess foam.

Step 6. Bring thread back to mid-section and attach black hackle.

Step 7. Wrap leg hackles and tie off.

Step 8. Whip finish and detach thread.

Step 9. Trim hackle flush with the bottom of the hook, This allows the fly to ride flat.

This pattern has proven extremely effective.

CICADA

Never having had occasion to fish the Cicada, I was introduced to this unique pattern by an excellent guide and fisherman on the Green River by the Flaming Gorge Dam. Dennis Breiar told me that if I wanted to have some real fun, just fish this black Cicada on the surface and let him know what I think. There was no question that Denny knew what he was talking about because the next day was one to remember. Since that day, I have fished this pattern as a Dark Hopper and a Cricket and have done equally well.

CICADA — Plate #14, Fly #14

Materials:
Hook: Tiemco TMC 101. Size 8-12
Body: Black Closed Cell Foam
Underbody: Black Ostrich Herl
Wing: White Calf Tail
Legs: Hackle Fiber
Hackle: Black
Thread: 6/0 Black Uni-Thread

Step 1. Attach thread and ostrich herl to the front section of the hook.

Step 2. Wrap thread to the rear, then wrap ostrich herl to the rear.

Step 3. Attach foam above the bend of the hook by wrapping 3 to 4 turns in the same place.

Step 4. Fold foam back, then wrap thread forward approximately 1/4 the length of the hook shank.

Step 5. Tie down foam using 3 to 4 wraps in the same place as in step 3.

Step 6. Fold foam back, then wrap thread forward.

Step 7. Snip off excess foam on a 45 degree angle, leaving a small amount to tie down.

Step 8. Attach calf tail wing.

Step 9. Attach hackle fiber legs on each side leaving 1/2 the length of the body past the back of the bend of the hook.
    The hackle fibers should be placed on the side with the natural bend of the fiber pointing outward. These fibers will act as stabilizers.

Step 10. Attach and wrap two black firm hackles.

Step 11. Tie small head and whip finish.

Step 12. Apply head cement.

P. C. HOPPER — Plate #14, Fly #6

Materials:
Hook: Mustad 94840; Tiemco TMC 101. Size 8-12
Body: Yellow Closed Cell Foam
Underbody: Red Ostrich Herl
Underwing: Deer Hair
Overwing: Nylon Reinforced Turkey Feather or Silk Imitation Flower Petal
Hackle: Brown
Legs: Hackle Fibers
Thread: 6/0 Dark

Step 1. Attach thread and red ostrich herl at the front of the hook.

Step 2. Bring thread to the rear and palmer ostrich herl the full length of the hook, tying off at the rear.

Step 3. Attach closed cell foam above the bend of the hook by wrapping 3 to 4 wraps in same place.

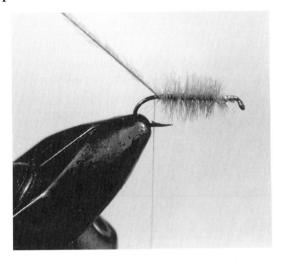

Step 4. Fold foam back, then wrap tying thread forward ¼ the length of the hook.

Step 5. Tie down foam with 3 to 4 wraps in same place.

Step 6. Fold foam back and wrap thread forward.

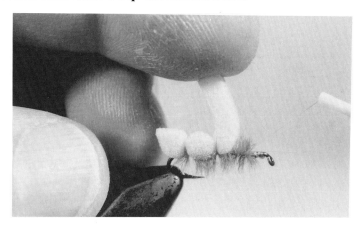

Step 7. Trim off front of foam at a 45 degree angle leaving a small area to tie down.

Step 8. Attach deer hair underwing.

Step 9. Strip fibers from two brown hackles and attach one on both sides. The fibers should extend back ½ the length of the body. The hackle fibers should be placed on the sides with the natural bend of the fiber pointing outward. These fibers will act as stabilizers.

Step 10. Prepare overwing from a petal off of a fake fern.

    a. Color fern petal with permanent marking pen.
    b. Detach petal from fern and fold in half.
    c. Cut petal, forming desired shape of wing.

    Note: This technique of wing making is ideal for stone flies as well.

Step 11. Attach overwing.

Step 12. Attach and wrap two brown firm hackles.

Step 13. Whip finish and apply head cement.

Step 14. Trim hackles flat on the underside, even with the bottom of the hook. This will allow the hopper to ride low — the legs will keep it from rolling over.

THE HUMPY

As originally tied, the only synthetic found in the Humpy was (possibly) the body material. Poly dubbing took the place of natural furs for the Humpy's body because of higher flotation characteristics. The tail and back were deer hair, the wings and hackle were natural feathers. Today, the Humpy is tied in a large number of variations, almost all of which include synthetics as the primary ingredients. Some unique ways of tying the Humpy are as follows.

POLY HUMPY — Plate #14, Fly #4

Materials:
Hook: Mustad 94840. Size 12-18
Body: Pale Yellow Floss
Tail: Brown Hackle Fibers
Back: Light Tan Synthetic Dubbing
Wings: Light Tan Synthetic Dubbing
Hackle: Brown – Same as Tail

Step 1. Attach Tail.

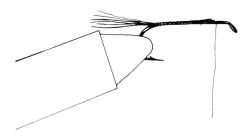

Step 2. Attach light tan dubbing to the hook leaving one and one-half times the hook shank length sticking out towards the back.

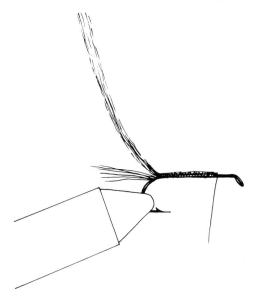

Step 3. Tie on floss and wrap thread to the front of the hook.

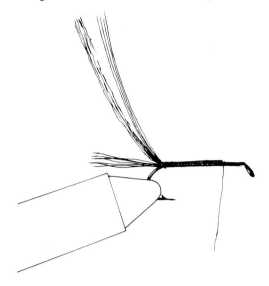

Step 4. Wrap floss body leaving two eye widths of clearance from the end.

Step 5. Pull over light tan dubbing as a shell back.

Step 6. Using excess material from the shell back separate and figure eight making wings.

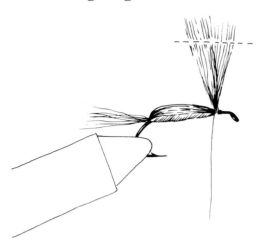

Step 7. Trim to shape and length.

Step 8. Attach brown hackle and tie off.

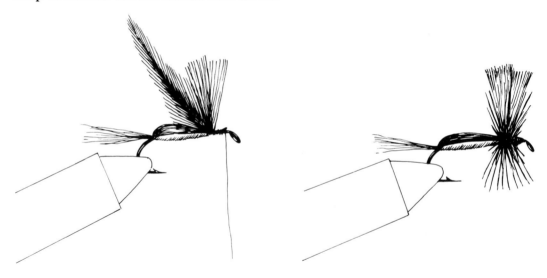

FOAM BACK HUMPY — Plate #14, Fly #7

This Humpy is tied exactly the same way as the Yellow Humpy except a piece of thin strip closed cell foam is used in place of the tan dubbing for shell back and body. If a piece of white foam is used, you can Pantone color the shell back and body and leave the excess white for the wings. This fly is very durable and once treated with a high quality floatant, will stay up forever.

THE HEATHEN

It seems as though the flies we use are getting smaller each year. Either that or I'm getting older and it's harder to see to tie them on. In the southwestern region of the Rockies, we have a large selection of midge patterns to choose from. Like in any other area, there are a certain few that really do the job on most any stream. The Heathen is one fly that I feel will fall in this category. Although still young and on trial, its performance and durability ranks among the top. This fly fits into the midge emerger category, and can bring home the bacon when fished anywhere from the river bottom to the top. It's successful in four feet or four inches of water, or in the middle of your favorite riff.

The Heathen came to life in Farmington, New Mexico during the Federation of Fly Fisherman Southwestern Conclave. I was asked to come down and demonstrate some of the different methods of tying with Larva Lace. About halfway through the first day, Mark Gruber came up to me and said "Let me show you how we are using your foam, we call this the bobbing emerger." Mark went on to show me the tying procedure of a fly soon to develop into the Heathen. This fly is Mark's bobbing emerger tied in the Heathen's color combination.

About 5:00 that afternoon, a few people were left mingling around and most of us tyers were starting to pack up and conclude our day with a nice meal supplied by the chapter. It was then that Rick Heath formerly of Rizuto's Flyfishing Store came over and said, "What's new Phil?" Well, I was impressed with Mark's bobbing emerger and I proceeded to show Rick. He said that he had been fishing that pattern on the San Juan River this summer and it had been real good, but that he was looking for a body color which he couldn't find. It was an iridescent green color he was looking for. We sat and went through a dozen combinations of materials to get it. When we did, there was no doubt in Rick's mind that he had it. That was the combination that would do the job on the San Juan and I was to try it ASAP.

Well, the following day Chuck Rizuto had taken me and a number of the guests up to Navajo Lake to tube for small mouth bass. I wasn't able to try out the pattern until I hit the South Platte River when I returned home. When I finally had the chance, we still had Tricos and midge Blue Wing Olives coming off each day. It sure didn't take long before my line stopped dead in the water and that great feeling of a 'fish on' took over. I found the Heathen to work best just under the surface. However, there was a period throughout the day when it was more productive at a submerged depth of 12″ in a run that was 24″ deep.

Since that Farmington Conclave, a number of my friends and I have been fishing this fly all over the southwestern Rockies with great success. I feel its productivity will remain and hope that it will give others the enjoyment it has given me.

HEATHEN — Plate #16, Fly #12

Materials:

Hook: Tiemco TMC 2457 or TMC 2487. Size 16-20

Underbody: One Wrap Pearl Krystal Flash

Body: Grey (#08) Larva Lace Slipped Over Krystal Flash, Segmented with Black 8/0 Uni-Thread

Wing: Upright- White Larva Lace Dry Fly Foam

Thorax: Coarse Hare's Ear, Dubbed Front and Back of Wing

Step 1. Tie on one piece of Krystal Flash, just behind the eye of the hook.

Step 2. When Krystal Flash is secured on hook, lift up, off the back of the hook and proceed wrapping hook shank with with black thread, stopping just at the bend of the hook.

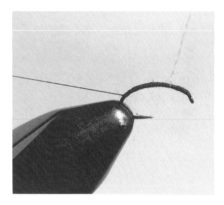

Step 3. Continue wrapping Krystal Flash over the shank of the hook, stopping at the bend.

Step 4. Tie off Krystal Flash and cut off remaining Krystal Flash material.

Step 5. Slip Larva Lace Body Material over the eye and shank of the hook, not to exceed half of hook shank.

Step 6. Snip Larva Lace at the eye of the hook and push remaining section back to bend of hook.

Step 7. Build small abdomen with tying thread and continue with close segmented wraps over the Larva Lace to the eye of the hook.

Step 8. Tie in small piece of closed cell foam approximately 1/3 shank length back from the eye of the hook. Leave foam pointing up as a parachute post.

Step 9. Dub coarse hare's ear in front and behind foam post, creating a thorax.

Step 10. Trim foam post short above hare's ear thorax when used as a nymph. Trim post high above the thorax when used as an emerger.

Other Patterns Which Feature Open Cell Foam:

River Witch (Pattern ref. pg. 45, 132   Plate 10, Fly 6)
Catalpa Worm (Pattern ref. pg. 53, 124   Plate 10, Fly 7)
Mini-Crawdad (Pattern ref. pg. 49, 129   Plate 11, Fly 4)
Streamers (Pattern ref. pg. 144-148   Plates 6 and 9)

IMPROVING DURABILITY

Improving the durability factor in your flies will not only make you a better fly tyer, it will also allow you to catch more fish. I say this because invariably your fly will decide to fall apart just when the hatch is at its peak and you drop the last like pattern you had in the stream while fumbling to get it tied on your line. That is only if you are lucky. If this has not happened to you yet, just wait until you drop your whole box in the stream. You will then be able to relate.

There are many ways of increasing the life of your flies and it helps to practice these as normal tying procedures. When tying on peacock herl bodies, wrap the peacock herl around the tying thread a number of turns before wrapping the herl around the hook shank. This will help prevent the herl from unraveling after you catch your first or second fish. If you want the peacock herl to last even longer, coat the hook shank with a light layer of head cement before wrapping. This will greatly increase the life of your fly.

When putting protective coatings onto fly bodies, a wide variety of products can be used. To protect mylar tubing, I use a thin layer of clear lacquer or a body coat of clear epoxy. Depending on what pattern and effect you are trying to obtain, both of these products work well. Another method of body protection is simply overwrapping with a clear protective coating such as translucent thread for very small flies or clear vinyl products for larger patterns. The following are examples of materials which work well for overwrapping larger patterns:

* Larva Lace body material
* Swannundaze
* Body Glass
* Nymph Rib
* Polybag strips

When tying in wings or tinsel fibers, make sure you lock them in by over-lapping at the tie in area if possible. Sometimes, because of excess bulk, the pattern will not lend itself to that. If it will not allow the overlap, put a drop of head cement down before tying in your material.

Many times you will take the extra step of finishing off your streamer or crustacean patterns by painting on some small eyes. The best protection you can give them is a light coat of clear lacquer. Make sure the eyes are dry before applying and make sure that the lacquer will not attack the product you used to paint on the eye.

Building Durability into Feathers

There are a couple of techniques I use to build durability into feathers. The feathers that have the most problems are turkey wings or tails when clipping them for wing cases or hoppers. Take an aerosol spray of clear lacquer and apply a couple of coats to the underside of the feather. You will be amazed at the strength you have just put into your material. Let the feather dry and slit out the sections you need as if it were untreated. This technique is great for helping you get your wing case tied on without splitting.

However, the material is still vulnerable to fish. To increase the feathers' durability even more, I use the nylon lamination technique. This technique is, by far, the best I know to maintain the original appearance and texture of the natural feather while building in the durability of a synthetic imitation. The easiest way to do this is as follows:

To begin, get a 10″ X 10″ piece of stiff cardboard. I call this a stretching board because I use this to stretch an old piece of light colored pantyhose the way you would stretch an animal skin.

Step 1. Stretch pantyhose tightly, completely covering the stretcher.

Step 2. Secure the pantyhose to cardboard with common pins.

Step 3. Insert a piece of wax paper between the pantyhose and cardboard.

Step 4. Coat the underside of your feather with aerosol contact cement.

Step 5. Coat pantyhose with light coat of contact cement.

Step 6. Wait the prescribed time according to the instructions on contact cement container, then press the two together.

Step 7. Trim off excess nylon and your reinforced feather is ready to use.

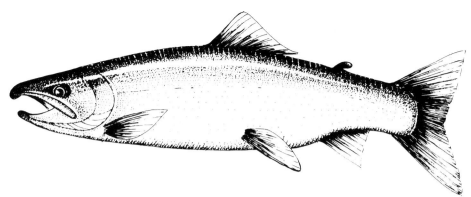

WEIGHTING THE WET FLY

There are many areas throughout the world that forbid the use of lead on your line, or tied into your fly. I suggest you become familiar with the regulations of the area that you intend to fish so that you will not fall into violation. If you find that situation exists,you may consider using a double hook design or tying materials that slip through the water easier. For example, a large stone fly tied with a chenille body will take a little longer getting down than a body tied with a slick non-resistant surface material. Do not be afraid to substitute standard material to obtain a faster sink rate. As long as you can hold a good simulation of the insect or food that you are trying to represent. The most important thing is to present it in the proper feeding zone. If that means getting the fly down, use some ingenuity as long as you stay within the law.

Where you learned to fly fish and how many articles you have read on weighting flys will determine what you have been doing in the past. You will find that you may weight the same pattern in a variety of ways depending on what fishery you are in and what your water flow conditions are. This is especially so in a tail water fishery where you can see a change in flow from day to day. As the water flow conditions change, so will the amount of weight needed to obtain natural drift or to bring you into the proper depth according to your chosen pattern.

Other reasons for weighting flys are to give them the proper swimming appearance if fished in still water. This will dictate where on the hook shank the weight is applied in order to give a forward or backward dipping effect when your line is stripped in.

When applying weight we may also be able to complete some other required steps in a given pattern. For example, a particular pattern may call for larger eyes and have a requirement for running deep. We can meet both of these requirements by using lead or bead chain eyes. The following weight applying techniques will give you the variety needed to weight most any type of fly.

LEAD WIRE WRAP

Pure lead wire comes in a variety of diameters, I seldom use a size of lead wire that is more than $1/2$ the diameter of the hook shank. This gives a fine, even appearance and allows for more gripping surface. The only time I wrap a larger diameter wire is when I intend to squeeze it down with pliers to form a body taper. In this case I will use a wire size that is equal to the hook shank.

Applying the wire wrap weight.

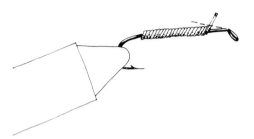

Using a flat surface pliers, squeeze the lead wire forming the desired taper. After lead is formed apply a light coat of head cement and lock lead body down tight with your tying thread

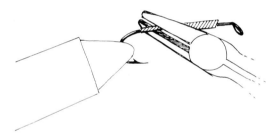

When a large amount of weight is needed we will apply the lead along both sides of the hook shank and one piece on the top.

This will also help from having body twist when plenty of weight is required. If a flat weighted body is all that is required, run the lead along both sides of the hook and tie in with your fly tying thread.

FLAT LEAD WRAP

Flat lead is becoming more and more popular, especially when tying large saltwater and salmon patterns. This type of material is desired because it lays down a large amount of lead without giving a large build up to the body. The whole secret to applying this lead is to not let it over-wrap itself. You want to take advantage of 100% gripping surface. Make each wrap lay just next to the other.

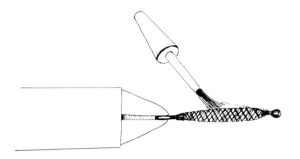

USING EYES FOR WEIGHT

When using eyes for weight, two types are most popular, lead and bead chain sections. (see Applying Eyes section – page 109)

SPLIT SHOT WEIGHTED FLIES

This is a technique used by Paul Drake and George Bodmer of Colorado Springs, Colorado when tying the Bullethead Muddler. The effect was to have a nose dipping action when the line was stripped.

   The actual technique of weighting was done by tying the standard muddler and crimping on a splitshot at the head area of the fly. Leave approximately $1/8''$ between the splitshot and the hook eye. Spin in a clump of deerhair and push back over the split shot. A rod ferrule was used as a tool to push the deer hair over the shot evenly. The deer hair was then tied down directly behind the head.

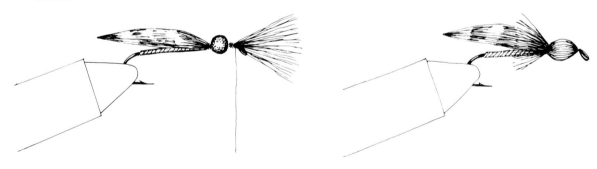

WEIGHTING THE DEER HAIR PERMIT CRAB FLY

The Deer Hair Permit Crab is a deer hair spun fly that is the shape of a $3/4''$ diameter wafer. The fly has eyes and claws giving the appearance of a sand crab. This fly is weighted by taking a length of lead wire and rolling it into the shape of a coin. When the lead is rolled, fasten it flat to the bottom of the crab with super glue and then apply white silicone caulking over the surface. Lead putty can be used in place of wire.

WEIGHTING THE WOOL CRAB

Although in appearance the Deer Hair and Wool Crabs can be made to look similar, the wool crab can be weighted with a soaking of fly sinking agent as well as with its water absorption qualities. Most of the wool crabs will also have a belly of silicon or hot glue to either add weight or give a different color to the crab's belly.

APPLYING EYES TO FLYS

When tying flies that require eyes it is important to choose the correct style and size to maintain proportion and realism. The eye you choose may also be considered for weight or attraction capability, dark or bright may be considered for water color or sun conditions. The following will introduce you to some of the many styles and techniques used to apply eyes to your flies.

PAINT EYES

When painting eyes you must choose a paint that is compatible with the surface you are painting over. If you are painting eyes on a surface that is non-compatible you may find that the paint will not set up or some chemical reaction might take place.

The simplest technique I know of is to get yourself a finishing nail and cut off the point end. The larger end is the one I use for the outer eye and the smaller for the pupil. By dipping the head of the finish nail into the paint (just enough to cover the flat surface) and placing it onto the face section of the fly, you can make perfectly round eyes the size of the nail head. Make sure when you pull back from the fly that the nail is fully separated from the point before moving to the other side. When the outer eye has dried, repeat the process with the smaller finishing nail, but with a different color paint.

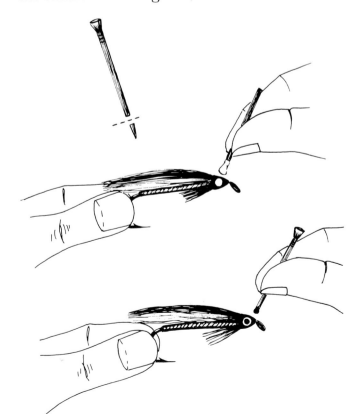

Paints most commonly used are: Epoxy Paints, Lacquer, Enamel

MONO EYE

Mono eyes are very unique and fun to make. Depending on the size of the fly will determine the size of the mono you will start with. If these eyes are used on small flies I make them as a set and tie them in as one set.

Example:

1. Hold a piece of .015 mono in a tweezers leaving ³/₈" hanging out from each side.

2. Use a cigarette lighter to burn back the mono, creating a round ball on each side.

3. Flatten the section of mono between the balls with a flat pliers or put it back in your tying vise. This flat section will allow you to tie in the eyes much more securely and with minimal build up.

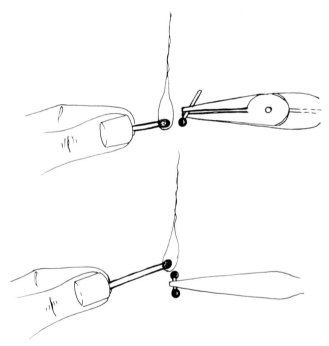

The length between the mono balls will be the section used to tie in the eyes. When tying these in you may find that it is easier to tie the eyes on first, then build up the rest of the fly around them. When tying the mono down to the hook it is best to have a few wraps of thread over the hook shank first. This gives a tighter gripping surface to the mono.

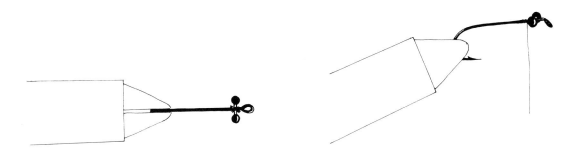

These eyes are tied on in a figure eight pattern.

When tying Mono eyes for Large Flies, I make them as a set, but tie them in individually. The following will explain.

1. Using a 2 inch piece of Mono, burn each end, creating the proper sized eye. Flatten down stem.

2. When attaching the eye to the fly, position one eyeball in the desired location and tie down the stem. When the stem is securely tied in, separate the other ball, set the Mono and position the remaining eyeball. Secure the other stem and cut off the remaining mono.

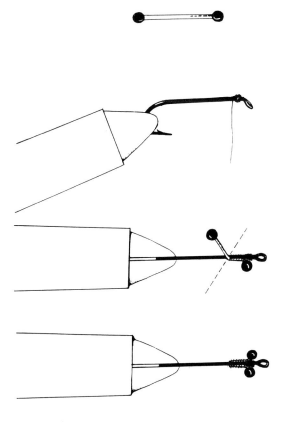

This is the procedure used in the crawdad pattern. (Ref. pps. 49-52)

MAKING AND ATTACHING THE LARVA LACE EYE

Combining the mono eye with a piece of Larva Lace body material produces an eye that has a lid and a pupil of different colors. The effect is quite interesting and the case of tying them to your fly makes this eye worth considering.

Step 1. Cut a piece of .015 dark color mono approximately 3 inches in length

Step 2. Cut a piece of Larva Lace Body Material approx. 1¹/₂″ in length.

Step 3. Insert Mono through the tubing leaving approximately ³/₄″ extending out of the opposite side.

Step 4. Proceed to burn the end of the mono until the desired pupil size is obtained.

Step 5. While the pupil is still burning, pull the opposite side of the mono through the Larva Lace.

When trying to pull the larger diameter pupil through the Larva Lace, the burning mono will melt and roll back the edge of the tubing. As continued pressure is applied to the mono the mono will separate from the pupil leaving it imbedded in the end of the Larva Lace. Let cool and attach to the fly. The soft end of the tubing will pull down to the fly easier than the hard mono eye.

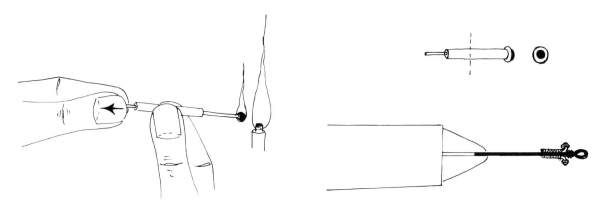

BEAD CHAIN EYES

When bead chain eyes became popular, it put all the electric light pull cords and bath tub stop chains in jeopardy. The search was always on at the junk fairs or flea markets to find the different sizes or colors. The most available sizes are small, medium and large with either a chrome or brass color finish. This style eye has become so popular that most all fly tying material suppliers will carry the chain. For eyes, simply cut between every other bead with a small wire cutter and separate each set of beads from the length. I find it convenient to have a small box of each size and color precut.

The installation of the bead chain eye is identical to the mono eye. When tying on the bead chain, attach it along the length of the hook. After making approximately 5 wraps the chain will turn on a 90 degree angle and self-position. Proceed by tying in with a figure eight pattern.

The advantages of the bead chain eye are:

1. Durability
2. Variety of color
3. Weight
4. Ease of attachment

See Sparkle Dunk Crazy Charlie pages 71-73.

THE LEAD EYE

The lead eye is a small hour glass shaped piece of lead. These eyes are available through many leading fly materials suppliers and come in a variety of sizes. Colors are gray and chrome.

If chrome or gray don't meet your fancy, these eyes lend themselves very nicely to painting. The painting procedure would be the same as painting Streamer eyes. You should use an undercoat of white primer before applying any other color. When holding the lead eye, a bobby pin comes in very handy.

The installation of lead eyes is very similar to the method used for bead chain eyes. The only change required is to leave a little more cushion between the eye and hook shank.

The first lead eyes were introduced by Tom Schumuecker of Wapsi Fly Co. in Mt. Home Arkansas. Through a joint effort between Lefty Kreh and Bill Hunter, many patterns have been developed and proven highly successful. Lead eyes are great for adding a lot of weight and increasing attraction capabilities.

I am presently tying a series of ice fishing flies using the lead eye. I call this pattern the Flig (fly-jig).

STAMEN EYES

While reading my Spring 1988 edition of *AMERICAN ANGLER & FLY TYER* I read an interesting and informative article by Anthony J. Route on Stamen eyes.

Route identifies Flower Stems as being the same appearance as burnt mono eye. These Stems are available in most craft shops and come in a variety of colors. However, there is one drawback.

According to Route, these Stems will deteriorate in water if not treated with a highly thinned solution of Aquaseal. Dip the entire Stamen into the thinned Aquaseal and place them on waxed paper.

When dry, use as burnt mono eyes.

PRISM TAPE EYES

These eyes are pre-cut dots of prism tape. They come about 200 to a sheet and are great for applying to jigs and large streamers. The P.C. Smelt (ref. Plate 6, Fly #3) is an example of prism tape eyes.

Application is easy, just stick the eyes on in the desired location. I highly recommend a couple of coats of thick head cement to insure adherence. Another option is to epoxy over eyes.

SUPPLIERS OF PRISM TAPE EYES:

Witchcraft Tape, Coloma, MI 49038
Phantom Tape Products, Carol Stream, IL

Reference Tables

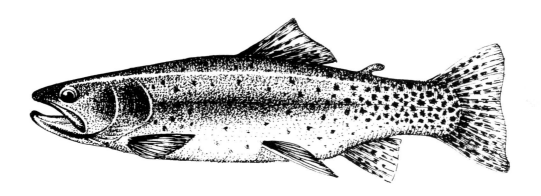

IDENTIFICATION GUIDE TO COLOR PLATES

TOOLS & MATERIALS

PLATE #1
1. Crystal Chenille
2. Metyllic Tinsel
3. Vinyl Paint
4. Poly Yarn
5. Rayon Floss
6. Imitation Fern
7. Fish Fuzz
8. Permanent Marking Pens
9. Crystal Hair
10. Lureflash Flat Pearl Mylar
11. Mylar Tubing
12. Angora Yarn
13. Rubber Legs
14. Larva Lace Nymph Rib
15. Fib-Etts
16. Fishhair
17. Swannundaze
18. Chenille
19. Micro Chenille
20. Prism Tape Eyes
21. Silver Bead Chain (cut)
22. 5 mm Pom-Poms (pre-made eggs)
23. Lead Eyes
24. Doll Eyes
25. Plastic Bead Chain
26. Danville Floss
27. Pre-made wing cases of imitation fern

PLATE #2
28. Lureflash Translucent
29. Flashabou
30. Larva Lace Body Material
31. Fly Sheet
32. Fly Sheet Wing Cutters
33. Antron
34. Nylon Stocking
35. Sparkletwist
36. Open Cell Foam
37. Closed Cell Foam
38. Synthetic Dubbing
39. Prism Tape
40. Sparkle Glitter
41. Synthetic Dubbing
42. Evazote (closed cell foam)
43. Sparkle Chenille
44. Ultra Hair
45. Translucent Thread (nylon)
46. Sparkle Flash

PLATE #3
1. Wing Cutter
2. Dubbit
3. Hackle Guards
4. Rotary Dryer
5. Fly Tyer's Vise
6. Wing Burners
7. Wing Cutting Pad
8. Fly Sheet Wing Cutter
9. Wing Grabber
10. Hackle Pliers
11. Scissors
12. Wing Cutter Inserts For #8
13. Boar Brush
14. Sewing Needle
15. Whip Finishing Tool
16. Hair Stacker
17. Head Cement applicators
18. Pliers
19. Jig Eye Paint remover
20. Tweezers
21. Front End of a Ball Point Pen used as a halfhitch tool
22. Single Edge Razor Blade
23. Thread Bobbin

TYERS CODES

The number next to the tyers names is that person's code. In the color plate index below, the tyers code number denotes who tied that particular fly.

1. Phil Camera
2. Rick Murphy
3. George Watkins
4. Roy Richardson
5. Chuck Rizuto
6. Dr. Fly (Jerry Berg)
7. Robert Ransom

8. Don Puterbaugh
9. Larry Walker
10. Bob Popovics
11. Greg Asbury
12. Frank Marcotte
13. Jason Volmer

INDEX TO COLOR PLATES OF FLYS

PLATE #4 – Fender Flies

Fly #	Fly Name	Tyers Code
1.	Fender Faced Deceiver	7
2.	Clear Vinyl Faced, Nylon Dressing Fender	7
3.	Side-Saddle Bucktail Fender	7
4.	Mylar-Faced Nylon Dressing Fender	7
5.	Bucktail Fender	7
6.	Mylar-Faced, Nylon Dressing Fender	7
7.	Side-Saddle Bucktail Bend-Back Fender	7
8.	Mylar-Faced Lefty's Deceiver Fender	7

PLATE #5 – Tarpon Flies (Apte style)

Fly #	Fly Name	Tyers Code
1.	Orange/Brown Hackle Grizzly	1
2.	Orange/Grizzly	1
3.	Yellow/ Grizzly	1
4.	Black/Red	1
5.	Pink Marabou	1

PLATE #6 – Streamers

Fly #	Fly Name	Tyers Code
1.	Surf Candy	10
2.	Lefty's Deceiver	1
3.	PC Smelt	1
4.	Blue Bend Back	11
5.	Glass Minnow Matuka	8
6.	Pink Bend Back	11
7.	Glass Minnow	8
8.	Tan Bend Back	11

PLATE #7 – Salmon Flies

Fly #	Fly Name	Tyers Code
1.	Flash Fly	2
2.	Flash Fly	2
3.	Everglow	2
4.	Everglow	2
5.	Sockeye, Pink	2
6.	Sockeye, Chartreuse	2
7.	Sparkle Shrimp	2
8.	Sparkle Shrimp	2

PLATE #8 – Steelhead Flies

Fly #	Fly Name	Tyers Code
1.	Pink Comet	2
2.	Purple Comet	2
3.	Larva Lace Aztec Spine Back	1
4.	Sparkle Dunk Charlie	1
5.	Krystal Bullet	2
6.	Krystal Bullet	2
7.	Winter Fly	2
8.	Skunk	2
9.	Purple Skunk	2
10.	Orange Butt Skunk	2
11.	Green Butt Skunk	2
12.	Polar Shrimp	2
13.	Pink Egg	1
14.	Double Egg	1
15.	Chartreuse Egg	1

PLATE #9 – Trout Streamers

Fly #	Fly Name	Tyers Code
1.	Synthetic Mickey Finn	1
2.	Senior Citizen	1
3.	Sparkle Wooly Bugger	2
4.	Egg Sucking Aztec Leach	1
5.	Adams Steelhead Fly	2
6.	Black Muddler	1
7.	Comet	2
8.	Alevin	2
9.	Boss	2
10.	Zonker	1

PLATE #10 – Trout Nymphs

Fly #	Fly Name	Tyers Code
1.	Bitch Creek	1
2.	Woven Damsel	6
3.	Woven Stone	9
4.	Black Stone	1
5.	Softback Stone	1
6.	River Witch	1
7.	Catalpa Worm	1
8.	Life-Like Caddis	5
9.	Deer Hair Scud	9
10.	Larva Lace Bread Crust Nymph	1
11.	Extended Body Nymph	8
12.	Marabou Scud	9

PLATE #11 – Crustaceans

Fly #	Fly Name	Tyers Code
1.	Hard Claw Camera's Crab	1
2.	Camera's Fiddler Crab	1
3.	Soft Claw Camera's Crab	1
4.	Mini Crawdad	1
5.	Epoxy Fly	1
6.	P.C. Shrimp	1

PLATE #12 – Bone Fish Flies

Fly #	Fly Name	Tyers Code
1.	Halfback Charlie (pearl)	1
2.	Halfback Charlie (yellow)	1
3.	Diamond Halfback	1
4.	Stinger	13
5.	Florida Sunrise	13
6.	Blind Diamond Halfback	1
7.	Brown Butt Bone Fish Fly	11
8.	Chico's Bone Fish Special	11
9.	Orange Butt Bone Fish Fly	11
10.	Blind PC Shrimp	1
11.	Pearl Standard PC Shrimp	1
12.	Tan PC Shrimp	1

PLATE #13 – Aquatic Worms and Larva

Fly #	Fly Name	Tyers Code
1.	San Juan Worm	1
2.	Micro Chenille San Juan Worm	1
3.	Loop Body San Juan Worm	1
4.	Aquatic Earthworm	1
5.	Cloudy Day San Juan Worm	1
6.	Gold Rib San Juan Worm	1
7.	Red San Juan Worm	1
8.	Bloodworm	1
9.	Red Chironomid	1
10.	Pink Chironomid	1
11.	Grey Chironomid	1
12.	Chartreuse Chironomid	1

PLATE #14 – Trout Dry Flies

Fly #	Fly Name	Tyers Code
1.	Adult Damsel Fly	9
2.	Extended Body May Fly	8
3.	Giant Hopper	1
4.	Poly Humpy	1
5.	Extended Body May Fly	8
6.	PC Hopper	1
7.	Foam Back Humpy	1
8.	Black Panther	3
9.	Henry's Fork Hopper	2
10.	Adams Humpy	1
11.	Adams	1
12.	Royal Renegade	4
13.	Tan Madame X	2
14.	Cicada	1
15.	Black Madame X	2
16.	Trico Spinner	1
17.	Red Ant	1
18.	Black Ant	1

PLATE #15 – Shrimp and Larva

Fly #	Fly Name	Tyers Code
1.	Light Crane Larva	1
2.	Pearl Shrimp	1
3.	Tan Shrimp	3
4.	Dark Crane Fly Larva	1
5.	Pink Shrimp	3
6.	Mysis Shrimp	1
7.	Brown Larva	1
8.	Olive Shrimp	3
9.	Poly Back Shrimp	1
10.	Caddis Larva	1
11.	Orange Shrimp	3
12.	Poly Back Shrimp	1

PLATE #16 – Soft Hackle Flies and Nymph and Emergers

Fly #	Fly Name	Tyers Code
1.	Royal Soft Hackle	1
2.	Silver Blue Soft Hackle	1
3.	Pheasant Tail Soft Hackle	1
4.	White Fish Fly	1
5.	Peacock Soft Hackle	1
6.	Caddis Soft Hackle	1
7.	Flashback Nymph	2
8.	Sparkle Nymph	2
9.	March Brown	1
10.	Sparkling Emerger	1
11.	Brown Sparkling Emerger	1
12.	Heathen	1
13.	Metallic Emerger	1
14.	Metallic Emerger	1
15.	Metallic Emerger	1

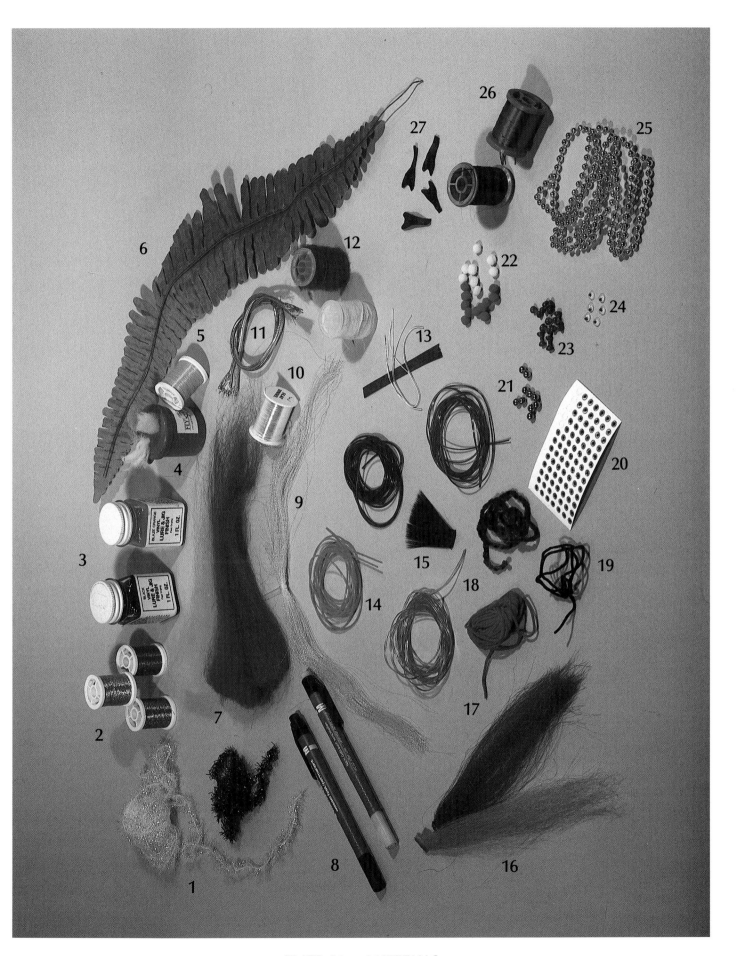

PLATE #1 — MATERIALS

PLATE #2 — MATERIALS

PLATE #3 — TOOLS

PLATE #4 — FENDER FLIES

PLATE #5 — TARPON FLIES (Apte Style)

PLATE #6 — STREAMERS

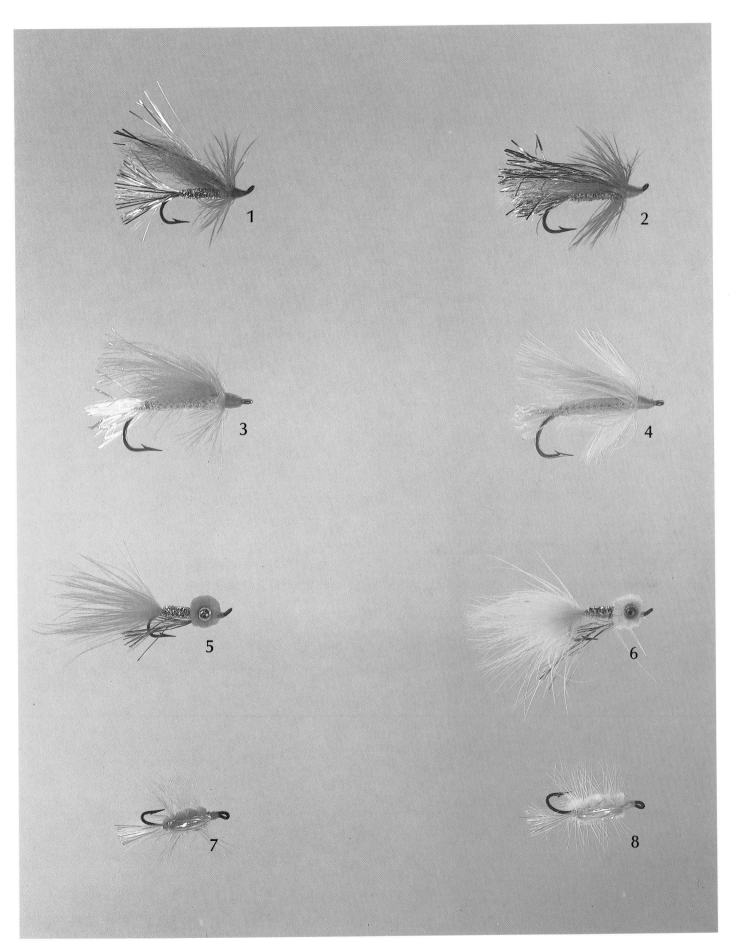

PLATE #7 — SALMON FLIES

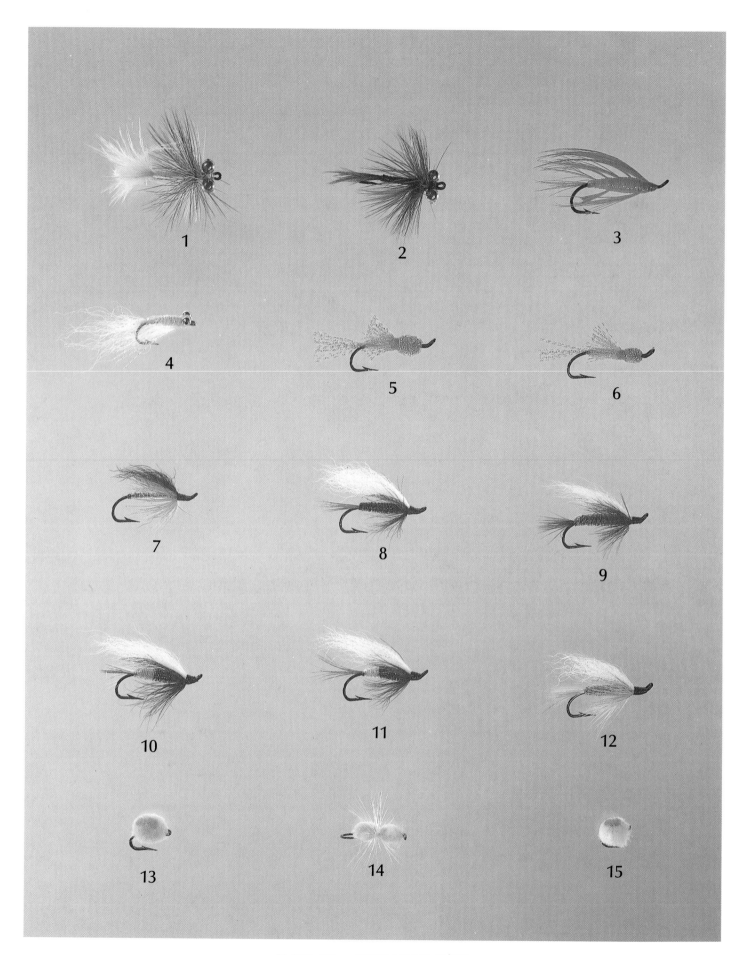

PLATE #8 — STEELHEAD FLIES

PLATE #9 — TROUT STREAMERS

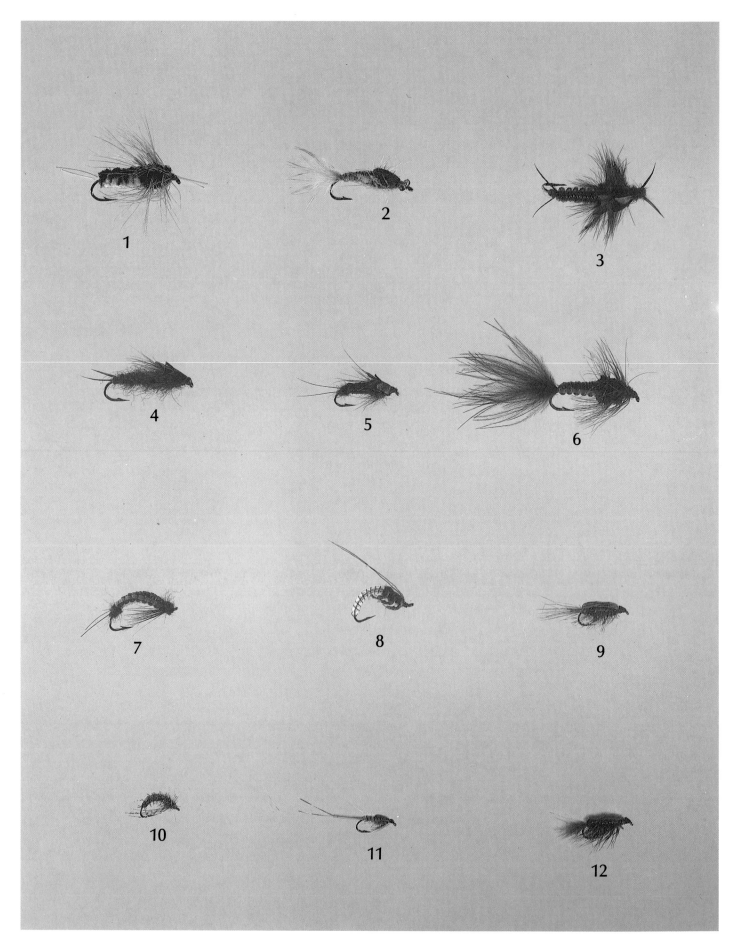

PLATE #10 — TROUT NYMPHS

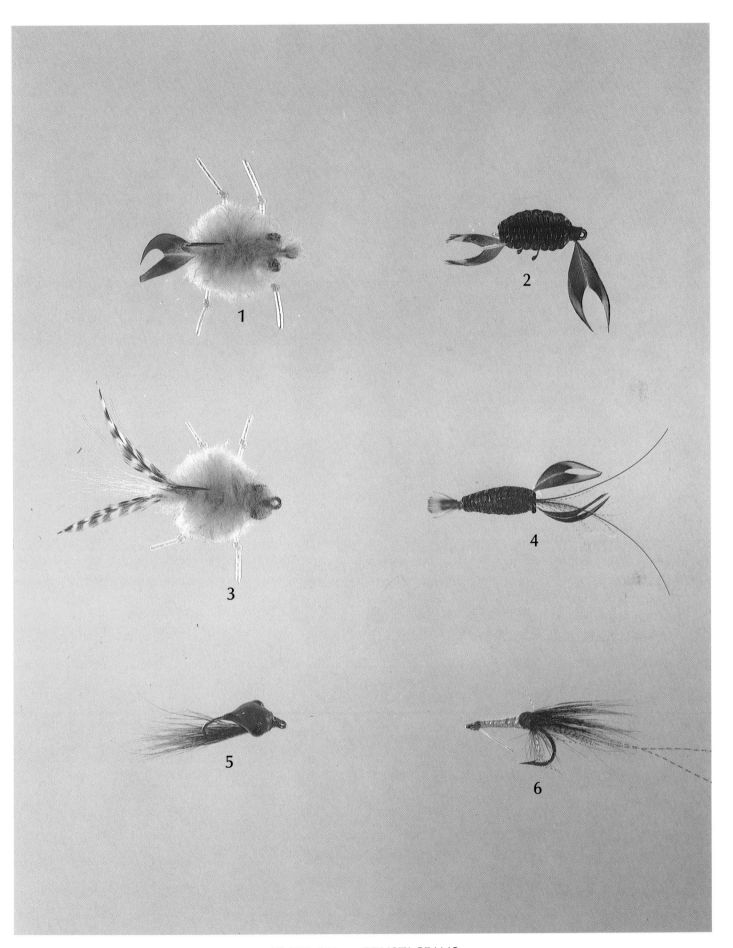

PLATE #11 — CRUSTACEANS

PLATE #12 — BONE FISH FLIES

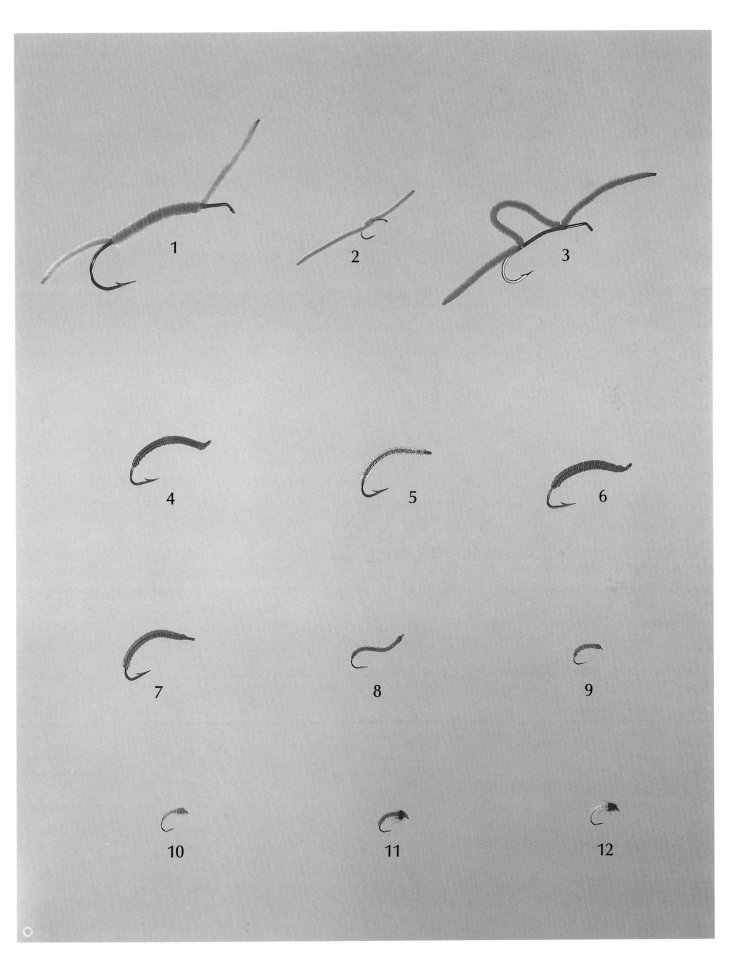

PLATE #13 — AQUATIC WORMS & LARVA

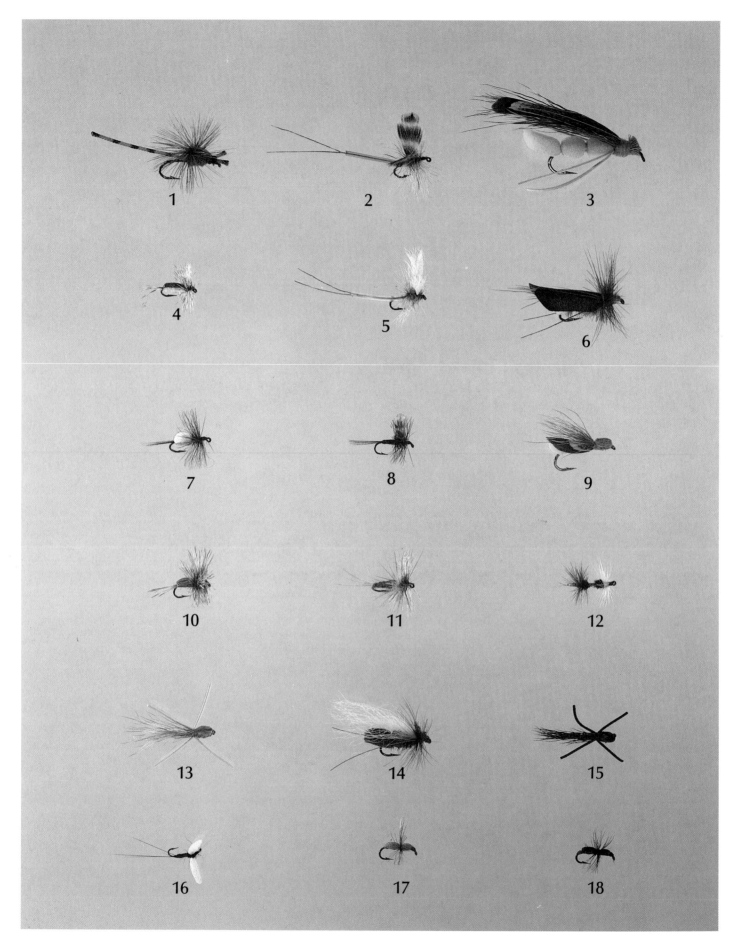

PLATE #14 — TROUT DRY FLIES

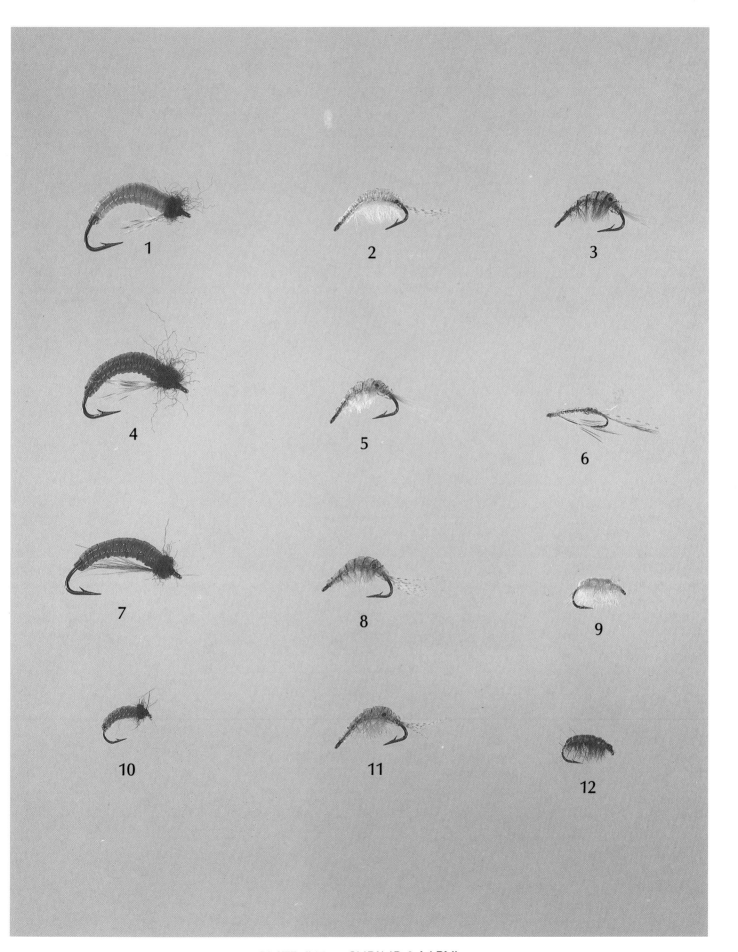

PLATE #15 — SHRIMP & LARVA

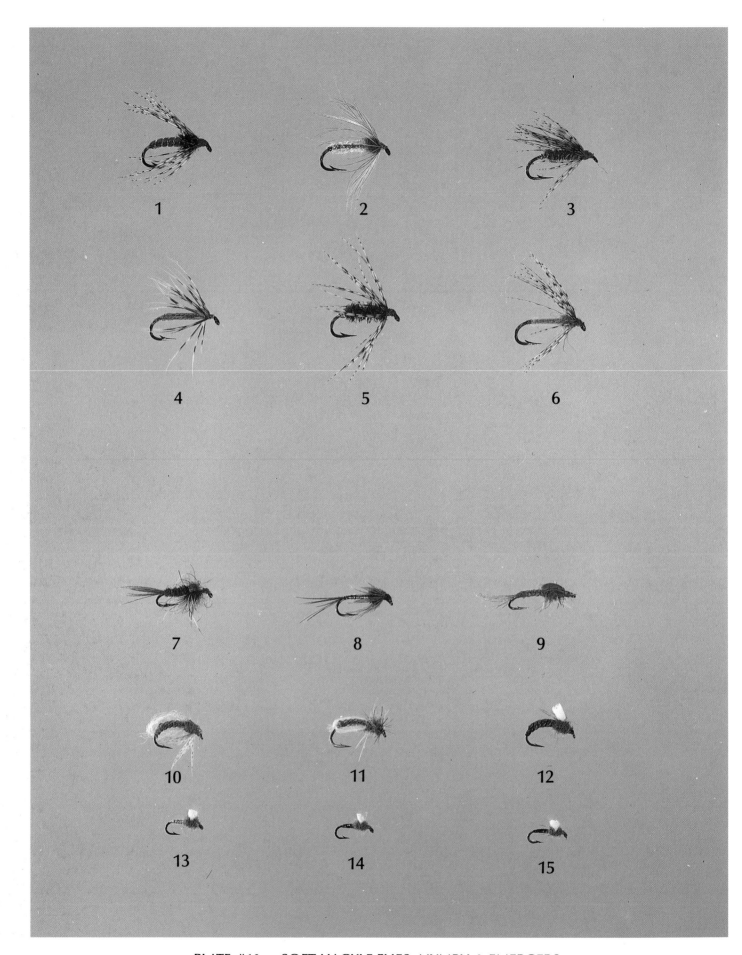

PLATE #16 — SOFT HACKLE FLIES, NYMPH & EMERGERS

FLY PATTERNS WITH SYNTHETICS

ADAMS STEELHEAD FLY

Hook: Mustad 36890
Tail: Brown Squirrel Tail
Body: Tan or Grey Dubbing over Lead Wire
Wing: Brown Squirrel Tail
Hackle: Grizzly Saddle
Thread: Yellow
Plate #9, Fly #5

ADULT DAMSEL FLY

Hook: Mustad 9671. Size 12 or 14
Thread: Black Mono or Larva Lace Translucent-Dark.
Abdomen: 25 or 30 lb. Braided Mono Dyed Blue. I used Veniard Cambridge Blue Dye.
Wing Case: Same as abdomen, tied back as loop, then pulled forward.
Hackle: Blue Dun Tied Parachute. Oversize.
Thorax: Dubbed Muskrat or any Grey Dubbing. Note: try a few wraps of Larva Lace Dry Fly foam in front of post before dubbing.
Eyes: Same piece as wing case after loop is pulled forward and clipped.
Marking Pen: Permanent black felt tip.
Plate #14, Fly #1

ALEVIN

Hook: Mustad 9671. Size 8-10.
Tail: Unraveled Pearl Mylar Tube
Body: Pearl Mylar Tube
Throat: Orange Marabou
Eyes: Large Chrome Bead Chain
Thread: Grey
Plate #9, Fly #8

AQUATIC EARTHWORM

Hook: Mustad 37160. Size 10.
Body: Brown (#02) Larva Lace Body Material
Collar: White Closed Cell Foam
Thread: Brown
Plate #13, Fly #4

AZTEC EGG-SUCKING LEACH

Hook: Mustad 36890 Limerick or Mustad 79580. Size 2-6
Tail: Black Marabou
Body: Larva Lace body material
Underbody: Larva Lace wet fly foam
Back: Black Marabou
Egg: Red Micro Chenille
Tie in small amount of Marabou on back after every 3rd wrap of larva lace.
Plate #9, Fly #4

AZTEC SPINE BACK

Hook: Mustad Limerick 36890. Size-6
Weighted body: Larva Lace LED
Underbody: Larva Lace wet fly foam
Body: Fluorescent Red (#06) Larva Lace body material
Spines: Dyed pheasant tail
Under Fins: Dyed pheasant tail
Tail: Dyed pheasant tail
Plate 8, Fly #3

BOSS

Hook: Mustad 36890. Size 6-10.
Tail: Black Calf Tail
Body: Black Chenille
Rib: Silver Metallic Tinsel
Hackle: Fluorescent Orange Saddle
Eyes: Large Chrome Bead Chain
Thread: Black
Plate #9, Fly #9

BITCH CREEK

Hook: Mustad 79580. Size 8-10.
Tail: White Rubber Strands (elastic)
Body: Black and Yellow Chenille
Thorax: Black Chenille
Hackle: Brown
Antenna: White Rubber Strands (elastic)
Plate #10, Fly #1

BLACK AND RED TARPON FLY

Hook: Mustad 34007. Size 3/0
Inner Tail: Black Calf Tail
Inner Wing: Black Saddle Hackle
Outer Wing: Black Saddle Hackle
Hackle: Red and Black Saddle Hackle mixed
Head: Black (#01) Larva Lace Body Material
Eyes: Black on Red Vinyl Paint
Plate #5, fly # 4

BLACK ANT

Hook: Mustad 94840. Size 14-18.
Body: Black Dry Fly Foam (strip)
Tab: Red Floss
Hackle: Black
Thread: Black 8/0 Uni-thread
Plate #14, Fly #18

BLACK AND PURPLE COMET

Hook: Mustad 36890
Thread: Black
Underbelly: Black Open Cell Foam
Overbody: Black (#01) Larva Lace Body Material
Tail: Purple Marabou
Hackle: Purple Saddle
Eyes: Silver Bead Chain
Plate #8, Fly #2

BLACK MADAM X

Hook: Mustad 94840. Size 12-14
Body: Pearl Mylar Tinsel
Tail: Black Deer Hair
Head: Black Deer Hair
Legs: Black Elastic Strands
Thread: 8/0 Uni-thread
Plate #14, Fly 15

BLACK MUDDLER MINNOW

Hook: Mustad 79580. Size 4-8
Tail: Red Hackle Fibers
Underbody: Pearl Mylar Tinsel
Body: Clear (#03) Larva Lace Body Material (overwrapped)
Wing: Black Deer Hair
Head: Black Deer Hair
Thread: Black
Plate #9, Fly #6

BLACK NOSE DACE

Hook: Mustad 79580. Size 6-12
Tail: Red Marabou (short piece)
Underbody: Silver Mylar
Body: Clear (#03) Larva Lace body material
Back: Gray squirrel Tail
Thread: Black Uni-Thread

BLACK PANTHER

Hook: Mustad 94840. Size 16-20
Body: Green Crystal Hair
Hackle: Black
Wings: Grizzly Hackle Tips
Thread: 8/0 Uni-thread
Plate #14, Fly #8

BLIND DIAMOND HALFBACK

Hook: Mustad 34007. Size 4-8.
Tail: Light Tan Marabou
Body: Larva Lace Body Material
Underbody weave: White Open Cell Foam covered with pearl mylar tinsel.
Halfback: Back – Chartreuse (#04) Larva Lace Body Material Belly – Clear (#03) Larva Lace Body Material
Thread: Tan
Note: Tie in a small piece of flat lead LED on the bottom side of the hook before starting to tie this fly. The weight will make this fly ride with the hook up
Plate #12, Fly #6

BLIND PC SHRIMP

Hook: Mustad 34007. Size 6-8.
Antenna: Orange Crystal Hair
Beard: Dyed Mallard Flank
Overbeard: Fox Squirrel Tail
Hackle: White
Eyes: Burnt Mono
Underbody: Pearl Mylar Tinsel
Body: Clear (#03) Larva Lace Body Material
Thread: Translucent
Plate #12, Fly #10

BLOOD WORM

Hook: TMC 400T. Size 12-14
Body: Orange (#10) Larva Lace Body Material (Slip over Method)
Rib: Red

Thread: 8/0 Uni-Thread
Use a slight amount of vegetable oil on the hook shank as a lubricant.
Plate 13 Fly #8

BLUE BEND BACK

Hook: Mustad 9353 ST
Body: Silver Mylar
Body Overwrap: Clear (#03) Larva Lace Body Material
Belly: White Bucktail
Back: Blue Bucktail with Silver Mylar Strips
Stripe: Grizzly Hackle on each side
Overback: Peacock Herl
Head: Blue Lacquer
Eyes: Black on White Lacquer
Plate #6, Fly #4

BONE FISH FLY

Hook: Mustad 34007 Stainless. Size 4-8
Tail: Orange Marabou – Short
Underbody: Pearl Mylar Tinsel
Body: Yellow (#13) Larva Lace body material (wrap method)
Beard: White calf tail with two grizzly hackle tips
Plate #12, Fly #8

BOSS – See page 121

BROWN DRAKE – DRY

Hook: Mustad 94840. Size 12-16.
Tail: Brown Hackle Fibers
Body: Reddish Brown Synthetic Poly Dubbing
Hackle: Brown
Wing: Grey
Thread: Brown 8/0 Uni-Thread

BROWN LARVA

Hook: Mustad 37160. Size 10-12.
Underbody: Open Cell Foam
Legs: Dark Hackle Fibers
Head: Black Rabbit (Coarse Dubbed)
Plate #15, Fly # 7

CADDIS LARVA

Hook: TMC 2487. Size 14-18
Body: Grey (#57) Larva Lace Nymph Rib
Head: Black Rabbit Fur (Dubbed)
Thread: 8/0 Black Uni-thread
Plate 15, Fly #10

CADDIS SOFT HACKLE

Hook: Mustad 3906B.
Body: Chartreuse (#04) Larva Lace Body Material
Ribbing: Nylon Translucent Thread
Collar: Hare's Ear
Plate #16, Fly #6

CAMERA'S CRAB (HARD CLAW)

Hook: Mustad 34007. Size 1/0
Claw: Pheasant Feather
Body: Light Tan Unspun Wool Legs: Larva Lace Body Material
Inner Legs: Orange Crystal Fibers
Eyes: Lead Eyes
Belly Adhesive: Hot Glue
Plate #11, Fly #1

CAMERA'S CRAB (SOFT CLAW)

Hook: Mustad 34007. Size 1/0
Claw: White Calf Tail with Grizzly Hackle on each side
Body: Unspun Wool
Legs: Larva Lace Body Material
Inner Legs: Orange Crystal Fibers
Eyes: Lead Eyes
Belly Adhesive: Hot Glue
Plate #11, Fly #3

CAMERA'S FIDDLER CRAB

Hook: Mustad 34007. Size 4.
Claws: Pheasant
Underbody: Lead Tape
Body: Brown (#02) Larva Lace Body Material (half hitch weave)
Eyes: Burnt Mono
Thread: Brown
Plate #11, Fly #2

CAMERA'S MYSIS SHRIMP

Hook: Tiemco 200R
Beard: Grizzly Fiber with a strand of Pearl Crystal Hair
Inner Body: Pearl Crystal Fiber wrapped around hook
Body: Clear (#03) Larva Lace Body Material
Eyes: Black Permanent Marker
Legs: Grizzly Hackle Fibers
Thread: Transluscent
Plate #15, Fly #6

CATALPA WORM

Hook: Mustad 37160. Size 8-10.
Tail: Black Hackle Fiber
Abdomen: Black Rabbit Dubbing
Underbody: Open Cell Foam
Legs: Black Hackle
Head: Black Rabbit Dubbing
Thread: Black
Plate #10, Fly #7

CHARTREUSE CHIRONOMID

Hook: Tiemco 2487. Size 16-20
Body: Fl. Chartreuse (#04) Larva Lace Body Material. (slipover method)
Collar: Black Rabbit (dubbed)
Thread: 8/0 Uni-thread
Plate #13, Fly #12

CHARTREUSE EGG

Hook: Mustad 9523.
Body: Chartreuse Poly Yarn
Inner Egg: Fluorescent Red Poly Yarn
Plate #8, Fly #15

CHARTREUSE SOCKEYE

Hook: Mustad 36890. Size 2-4.
Tail: Marabou, same color as head
Thread: Chartreuse
Body: Gold Polyflash
Eyes: Silver Bead Chain
Head: Chenille
Throat: Flashabou
Plate # 7, Fly #6

CICADA

Hook: Mustad 94831.
Legs: Black Ostrich
Body: Black Closed Cell Foam (sheet)
Outriggers: Hackle Fibers
Wing: White Calftail
Hackle: Black
Plate #14, Fly #14

CLOUDY DAY SAN JUAN WORM

Hook: Mustad 37160. Size 10
Body: Shrimp Color (#12) Larva Lace Body Material with Orange Crystal Hair inserted through it.
Thread: Nylon Translucent.
Plate #13, Fly #5

COMET

Hook: Mustad 36890. Size 6-10.
Tail: Orange Hackle Fibers
Body: Gold Poly Flash
Hackle: Red and Orange
Eyes: Large Brass Bead Chain
Thread: Orange
Plate #9, Fly #7

CRANE FLY LARVA

Hook: Mustad 37160 (Bend out 50% of Curve). Size 6-14
Underbody: Open Cell Foam
Body: Larva Lace Body Material
Colors: Grey, Olive, Red-Brown, Yellow. Use different color underbodies to get proper finish effect.
Thread: 4/0 Uni-thread
Plate 15, Flies #1, #4, #7

CRAZY CHARLIE

Hook: Mustad 34007 (Stainless Steel). Size 4-6
*****Tail:** White Calf Tail (Krystal Flash)
Underbody: Pearl Mylar
Body: Clear (#03) Larva Lace Body Material (Wrap Method)
*****Beard:** Krystal Flash & Calf Tail
Eyes: Bead Chain
Thread: White 6/0 Uni-thread
*Krystal Flash color should be same as body.
Plate #8, Fly #4

DAMSEL FLY NYMPH

Hook: Mustad 79580. Size 12-16
Body: Larva Lace Nymph Rib (green, #56)
Tail: Peacock Spears
Wing Case: Swiss Straw (Green)
Thorax: Olive Ostrich Herl
Eyes: Burnt Mono
Thread: Larva Lace Clear Translucent (Ultra Fine)

DARK CRANE FLY LARVA

Hook: Mustad 37160. Size 8-12
Underbody: Dark Open Cell Foam Strip
Body: Olive (#09) Larva Lace Body Material
Legs: Grizzly Fibers
Head: Black Rabbit (Coarse Dubbed)
Plate #15, Fly #4

DEER HAIR SCUD

Hook: 3906 B
Body: Brown (#02) Larva Lace Body material
Legs: Olive Ostrich
Tail: Olive Deer Hair
Back: Olive Deer Hair
Thread: Black
Plate #10, Fly #9

DEER WING HUMPY

Hook: Mustad 94840. Size 12-16.
Body: Poly Synthetic Dubbing
Tail: Deer Hair
Back: Deer Hair
Wing: Deer Hair
Hackle: Grizzly and Brown Hackle
Thread: 8/0 Uni-thread
Plate #14, Fly #10

DIAMOND BACK

Hook: Mustad 34007. Size 4-8.
Tail: Fox squirrel Tail
Underbody: Pearl Mylar Tinsel
Body/Back: Brown (#02) Larva Lace Body Material
Body/Belly: Clear (#03) Larva Lace Body Material
Eyes: Chrome Bead Chain Eyes
Thread: Brown
Plate #12, Fly #3

DOUBLE EGG

Hook: Mustad 3609 B. Size 8-14.
Body: Pink Poly Yarn
Inner Egg: Yellow Poly Yarn
Hackle: White
Plate #8, Fly #14

DRAGON FLY NYMPH

Hook: TMC 5262 or 3906B. Size 10-14
Tail: Peacock Spears (2)
Underbody: Dark Fly Tying Foam (Wet)
Thorax: Peacock Herl
Body: Olive (#09) Larva Lace Body Material
Legs: Peacock Herl
Wing Case: Dark Reinforced Silk or Turkey Feather
Thread: 6/0 Uni-Thread

EARTH WORM

Hook: Mustad 37160. Size 2-6 (Straighten out 50% of Bend)
Body: Larva Lace Body Material (Wrap Method)

Color: Red-Brown
Collar: White Larva Lace Fly Tying Foam (Dry)
Thread: 4/0 Brown Uni-thread
Plate 13, Fly #4

EMERGER – Black

Hook: Tiemco 100. Size 18-22
Body: Nylon Translucent Thread covered with permanent marker.
Thorax: Muskrat
Wing: Larva Lace Dry Fly Foam
Plate #16, Fly #15

EPOXY FLY

Hook: Mustad 34007. Size 1/0
Body: 5 Minute Epoxy
Eyes: Burnt Mono
Claw: Fox Squirrel Tail
Plate #11, Fly #5

EVERGLOW FLY

Hook: Mustad 34007 or Mustad 36890.
Thread: Same color as wings
Underbody: White Open Cell Foam
Body: Everglow Tubing
Underwing: Calf Tail to match Body Color
Wing: Unwoven Everglow Tubing Strands
Plate #7, Flies #3 & #4

EXTENDED BODY MAY FLY

Hook: Mustad 94836. Size 12-16
Tail: Hackle Stems
Body: Olive (#09) Larva Lace Body Material
Wing: Grizzly Tips
Hackle: Grey
Thread: 8/0 Uni-thread
Plate #14, Fly #2

EXTENDED BODY NYMPH

Hook: Mustad 3906. Size 14.
Tail: Grizzly Hackle Stems
Body: Larva Lace Body Material
Thorax: Dubbed Hare's Ear
Legs: Hackle Fibers
Wing Case: Turkey Feather
Thread: Black
Plate #10, Fly #11

FALL FAVORITE
Hook: Mustad 39890. Size 4-8
Tail: Red Hackle Fiber
Underbody: Silver mylar
Body: Clear (#03) Larva Lace body material
Hackle: Red Saddle Hackle
Wing: Red/Brown calf tail
Thread: 4/0 black Uni-thread

FLASHBACK NYMPH
Hook: Tiemco 5262 or Mustad 3906B. Size 12-16
Tail: Pheasant Tail Fibers
Body: Dubbed Hare's Ear
Ribbing: Fine Gold Metallic Tinsel
Thorax: Hare's Ear
Wing Cases: Pearl Mylar Tinsel
Thread: Black 6/0
Plate #16, Fly #7

FLASH FLY, ORANGE HEAD
Hook: Mustad 34007 or Mustad 36890. Size 3/0 or 4/0
Thread: Orange
Tail: Silver Flashabou
Body: Silver Polyflash
Wing: Silver Flashabou
Back: Orange Calf Tail
Hackle: Red Saddle
Plate #7, Fly #2

FLASH FLY, RED HEAD
Hook: Mustad 34007 or Mustad 36890. Size 3/0-4/0
Thread: Red Monocord
Tail: Silver Flashabou
Body: Silver Polyflash
Wing: Silver Flashabou
Back: Red Calf Tail
Hackle: Orange Saddle
Plate #7, Fly #1

FLORESCENT MARABOU STREAMER
Hook: Mustad 34007 or Mustad 36890. Size 4-10
Underbody: Larva Lace fly tying foam (yellow)(wrap method)
Body: Larva Lace body material (fluorescent)
Back: Marabou same color as florescent body material with black Marabou over the top
Thread: 3/0 black Uni-thread

FLUORESCENT PINK SOCKEYE
Hook: Mustad 36890. Size 2-4
Thread: Same color as head
Body: Silver Polyflash
Eyes: Silver Bead Chain
Head: Chenille
Throat: Flashabou
Tail: Marabou, same color as head
Plate #7, Fly #5

FLORIDA SUNRISE
Hook: Mustad 34007. Size 2-6.
Tail: Golden Pheasant Crest
Underbody: Yellow Monocord
Body: Clear (#03) Larva Lace Body Material
Eyes: Small Lead Eyes
Thread: Danville Yellow
Plate #12, Fly #5

FOAM BACK HUMPY
Hook: Mustad 94840. Size-12-18
Body: Closed Cell Foam
Tail: Brown Hackle Fibers
Back: Closed Cell Foam
Wings: Light Tan Synthetic Dubbing
Hackle: Brown – Same as Tail
Plate #14, Fly #7

GIANT HOPPER
Hook: Mustad 94881. Size 4-6.
Body: Evazote Closed Cell Foam
Thread: Same color as body
Stabilizers: Rubber Fibers (elastic)
Underwing: Deer Hair
Overwing: Pheasant (church window)
Plate #14, Fly #3

GLASS MINNOW
Hook: Mustad 91615 or 92616
Underbody: Yellow Open Cell Foam
Stripe: Silver Mylar
Overbody: Clear (#03) Larva Lace Body Material
Tail: White Marabou
Back: Fox Squirrel Tail
Plate #6, Fly #7

GLASS MINNOW MATUKA
Hook:
Underbody: Yellow Open Cell Foam
Stripe: Silver Mylar
Body Overwrap: Clear (#03) Larva Lace

Tail: White Marabou
Back: Fox Squirrel Tail
Plate #6, Fly #5

GOLDEN DEMON
Hook: Mustad 36890. Size 4-8
Tail: Gold or Yellow Hackle Fibers
Underbody: Gold mylar
Body: Clear (#03) Larva Lace (wrap method)
Collar: Gold or yellow dubbed Rib
Hackle: Gold and red saddle hackle
Wing: Goldish orange calf tail
Thread: 3/0 black or Black Mono Cond.

GOLDEN STONE NYMPH
Hook: 7957B. Size 8-12
Body: Dyed Rabbit Fur (Gold Yellow Color)
Rib: Yellow (#13) Larva Lace Body Material or
Yellow Nymph Rib
Wing Case: Dyed latex or Swiss Straw —Golden
Brown
Thorax: Dyed Rabbit

GOLD RIBBED SAN JUAN WORM
Hook: Mustad 37160. Size 10
Body: Red (#14) Larva Lace Body material
Ribbing: Gold Metallic Tinsel
Plate #13, Fly #6

GREEN BUTT SKUNK
Hook: Mustad 36890. Size 4-6
Tail: Red Hackle Fibers
Underbody: Green and Black Floss
Body: Clear (#03) Larva Lace Body Material
Hackle: Black
Wing: White Calf Tail
Plate #8, Fly #11

GREY CHIRONOMID
Hook: Tiemco 2487. Size 16-20
Body: Grey (#08) Larva Lace Body Material
(slipover method)
Collar: Black Rabbit (dubbed)
Thread: 8/0 Uni-thread
Plate #13, Fly #11

HEATHEN
Hook: Tiemco 2487 or Daiichi
Underbody: Pearl Crystal Hair Fiber over Black
Thread
Body: Grey (#08) Larva Lace Body Material
Ribbing: 8/0 Uni-thread

Thorax: Hare's Ear
Wing: Larva Lace Dry Fly Foam
Plate #16, Fly #12

HELLGRAMMITE
Hook: TMC 5262 or 3906B. Size 8-14
Tail: Black Biot (Goose Quill)
Underbody: Larva Lace Fly Tying Open Cell
Foam
Body: Black (# 01)Larva Lace Body Material
Ribbed Black Ostrich between Larva Lace
Segments
Thorax: Black Angora Yarn
Hackle: Black
Wing Case: Goose Feather (Inked Black)
Throat: Red Yarn
Thread: 4/0 Black

HENRY'S FORK HOPPER
Hook: Mustad 94840. Size 10-14
Body: Yellow Larva Lace Dry Fly Foam
Underwing: Pheasant Feather
Head and Overwing: Deer Hair
Thread: 6/0 Uni-thread
Plate #14, Fly #9

LARVA LACE BITCH CREEK
Hook: Mustad 3906B. Size 8-12
Tail: White elastic strip
Underbody: Larva Lace Fly Tying Foam (Wet)
*Body: Larva Lace Body Material (Weave
Method)
Back: Body Material Black
Belly: Yellowish Orange Chenille
Hackle: Black Hackle
Thorax: Black Chenille
Thread: 4/0
*Popular colors are: Black Back w/Orange Belly
and Black Back w/Yellow Belly
Plate 10, Fly #1

LARVA LACE BREAD CRUST
Hook: Mustad 37160 or Eagle Claw 141
Underbody: Brown Floss
Body: Orange (#10) Larva Lace Body Material
Rib: Brown Hackle trimmed close to stem
Thorax: Dubbed Hare's Ear
Legs: Partridge
Plate #10, Fly #10

LARVA LACE CRAWDAD (LARGE)

Hook: Mustad 37160. Size 2-6
Beard: Mallard Flank Feathers
Eyes: Burnt Mono
Claws: Pheasant Breast Feathers
Antenna: Black Hackle Stems
Head: Brown Chenille
Hackle: Brown
Back of Head: Swiss straw and latex
Underbody: Larva Lace Fly Tying Foam (Wet)
Body: Larva Lace Body Material
Tail: Swiss straw or Latex

LARVA LACE GLASS MINNOW STREAMER

Hook: Mustad 79580 or Mustad-Stainless 34007. Size 4-10
Body: Clear (#54) Larva Lace Nymph Rib (wrap over bear hook)
Back: White Fishair with peacock strands on top with chartreuse Fishair on top of peacock strands.
Thread: 4/0 black Uni-thread

LEFTY'S DECEIVER

Hook: Mustad 34007. Size 2-4/0.
Body: Silver Crystal Chenille
Back: White Saddle Hackle
Overback: Peacock Herl
Eyes: Yellow Prism Tape Eyes
Throat: Red Saddle Fibers
Plate #6, Fly #2

LIFE LIKE CADDIS

Hook: Mustad 37160. Size 10-12.
Underbody: Green Floss
Body: Clear (#03) Larva Lace Body Material
Ribbing: Fine Copper Wire
Thorax: Dark Brown Beaver Dubbing
Legs: Coated Copper Wire
Antenna: Moose Hair
Thread: Black
Plate #10, Fly #8

LIGHT CRANE FLY LARVA

Hook: Mustad 37160. Size 8-12
Underbody: White Open Cell Foam
Body: Olive (#09) Larva Lace Body Material
Legs: Grizzly Fibers
Head: Black Rabbit Coarse Dubbed
Plate #15, Fly #1

LOOP BODY SAN JUAN WORM

Hook: Tiemco 2457
Body: Ultra Chenille
Thread: Red, or same color as chenille
Plate #13, Fly #3

MARABOU SCUD

Hook: Mustad 3906B. Size 12-14.
Tail: Olive Marabou
Back: Olive Marabou
Body: Olive (#09) Larva Lace Body Material
Legs: Olive Hen Hackle
Thread: Black
Plate #10, Fly #12

MARCH BROWN NYMPH

Hook: Tiemco 5262 or Mustad 3906B. Size 16-18
Tail: Pheasant Tail Fibers
Wing Case: Pheasant Tail
Body: Brown (#02) Larva Lace Body Material
Rib: Nylon Translucent Thread
Thorax: Hare's Ear
Thread: Brown
Plate #16, Fly #9

MAY FLY NYMPH

Hook: TMC 5262. Size 12-18
Body: Larva Lace Body Material (Slip Over Method)
Ribbing: Clear Translucent Tying Thread (Ultra Fine)
Wing Case: Pheasant Tail or Flash Material
Thorax: Dubbed Rabbit Hair or Marabou
Tail: Pheasant Tail Fibers
Plate 16, Flies #7, #8, #9

METALLIC EMERGER – Gold

Hook: Tiemco 100. Size 18-22
Underbody: Fine Gold Metallic Tinsel
Body: Nylon Translucent Thread (Overwrap)
Thorax: Muskrat
Wing: Larva Lace Dry Fly Foam
Plate #16, Fly #13

MICRO-CHENILLE SAN JUAN WORM

Hook: Tiemco 2457
Body: Micro-chenille
Thread: Tan
Plate #13, Fly #2

MIDGE LARVA

Hook: TMC 2487 or 2457. Size 14-18
Body: Larva Lace Body Material (Slip Over Method)
Head: Block-Dubbed Rabbit Fur
Thread: Larva Lace Translucent Clear (Ultra Fine)
Plate 13, Flies #10, #11, #12

MYSIS SHRIMP

Hook: TMC 2487; Size 16-22
Beard: Grizzly hackle fibers
Body: Clear (#54) Larva Lace Nymph Rib
Eyes: Black indelible ink
Legs: Grizzly hackle

MINI CRAWDAD

Hook: Mustad 37160. Size 6-8
Beard: Pheasant Tail
Eyes: Burnt Mono
Claws: Ring Necked Rooster/Pheasant Breast Feather
Underbody: Larva Lace Fly Tying Foam (Wet)
Body: Larva Lace Body Material
Tail: Hen Hackle
Plate 11, Fly #4

OLIVE SHRIMP

Hook: Mustad 37160 or Eagle Claw 141
Body: Green (#07) Larva Lace Body Material
Legs: Olive Ostrich
Beard: Dyed Mallard Flank
Eyes: Black Permanent Marker
Thread: Nylon Translucent Thread
Plate #15, Fly #8

ORANGE/BROWN GRIZZLY TARPON FLY

Hook: Mustad 34007. Size 3/0
Inner Tail: White Marabou
Wings: Grizzly Saddles
Hackle: Brown and Grizzly Head: Orange (#10) Larva Lace
Thread: Red Uni-thread
Eyes: Black on White or Yellow, Vinyl Paint
Plate 5, Fly #1

ORANGE BUTT BONE FISH FLY

Hook: Mustad 34007. Size 4-8
Body: Fluorescent Orange (#05) Larva Lace Body Material – Fluorescent Pink (#06) Larva Lace Body Material

Eyes: Glass
Back: Grey Squirrel Tail
Thread: Fluorescent Pink
Plate #12, Fly #9

ORANGE BUTT SKUNK

Hook: Mustad 36890. Size 4-6
Tail: Red Hackle Fibers
Underbody: Orange Floss and Black Floss
Body: Clear (#03) Larva Lace Overwrap
Hackle: Black Hackle
Wing: White Calf Tail
Thread: Black
Plate #8, Fly #10

ORANGE GRIZZLY TARPON FLY

Hook: Mustad 34007. Size 3/0
Inner Tail: Orange Calf Tail
Inner Wing: Grizzly Saddle
Outer Wing: Orange Saddle
Hackle: Orange and Grizzly mix
Head: Fluorescent Orange (#05) Larva Lace Body Material
Thread: Red Uni-thread
Eyes: Black over White or Yellow Vinyl Paint
Plate #5, Fly #2

ORANGE KRYSTAL BULLET

Hook: Mustad 36890. Size 4-8.
Thread: Fluorescent Orange
Underbody: Open Cell Foam
Body: Fluorescent Orange (#05) Larva Lace Body Material
Tail: Orange Krystal Flash
Head: Orange Krystal Flash
Wing: Orange Krystal Flash
Plate #8, Fly #6

ORANGE SHRIMP

Hook: Mustad 37160 or Eagle Claw 141. Size 14-16
Beard: Dyed Mallard Flank Body: Orange (#10) Larva Lace Body Material
Eye: Black Permanent marker
Plate #15, Fly #11

P.C. HOPPER

Hook: Mustad 94831. Size 8-10
Underbody: Red Ostrich
Body: Yellow Larva Lace Dry Fly Foam (sheet)
Underwing: Deerhair
Overwing: Fake Fern Dyed Brown
Hackle: Brown
Outriggers: Dark Brown Hackle stems
Thread: Yellow
Plate #14, Fly #6

P.C. SHRIMP

Hook: Mustad 34007. Size 2-6
Antenna: Orange Crystal Hair
Beard: Dyed Mallard Flank
Overbeard: Fox Squirrel Tail
Hackle: Brown
Eyes: Lead Eyes
Underbody: Tan Floss
Body: Shrimp Color (#12) Larva Lace Body Material
Weed Guard: 18# test Mono, looped
Plate #11, Fly #6

P.C. SMELT

Hook: (Saltwater) Mustad 92608. Size 4. (Freshwater) Mustad 94720.
Tail: White Marabou
Underbody: Open Cell Foam
Underbody Cover: Pearl Mylar
Body: Clear (#03) Larva Lace Body Material(half-hitch weave)
Eyes: Yellow Prism Tape
Thread: Translucent
Plate #6, Fly #3

PEACOCK SOFT HACKLE

Hook: Tiemco 5262, Mustad 3906B. Size 12-16
Tab: Gold Metallic Tinsel
Body: Peacock Herl
Hackle: Partridge
Thread: Black
Plate #16, Fly #5

PEARL HALFBACK CHARLIE

Hook: Mustad 34007. Size 4-8
Tail: White Calf Tail
Underbody: Underbody is a serpent heading
Underbody: Pearl Mylar Tinsel
Body: Clear (#03) Larva Lace Body Material
Underweave: Open Cell Foam
Back: White Calf Tail with Pearl Crystal Fibers mixed in
Eyes: Chrome Bead Chain
Thread: Nylon Translucent
Plate #12, Fly #1

PEARL SHRIMP

Hook: Mustad 37160 or Eagle Claw 141. Size 14-16
Body: Clear (#03) Larva Lace Body material
Beard: Grizzly Fibers
Legs: White Ostrich
Thread: Nylon Translucent
Eyes: Permanent Black Marker
Plate #15, Fly #2

PHEASANT TAIL SOFT HACKLE

Hook: Tiemco 5262 or Mustad 3906B. Size 12-16
Tab: Gold Metallic Tinsel
Body: Pheasant Tail Wrapped around Gold Tinsel
Hackle: Partridge
Thread: 8/0 Uni-thread
Plate #16, Fly #3

PINK AND PURPLE COMET

Hook: Mustad 36890
Thread: Pink
Underbody: White Open Cell Foam
Overbody: Pink (#06) Larva Lace Body Material
Tail: Pink Marabou
Hackle: Pink Saddle & Purple Saddle
Eyes: Silver Bead Chain
Plate #8, Fly #1

PINK BEND BACK

Hook: Mustad 9353 ST.
Body: Silver Mylar
Body Overwrap: Clear (#03) Larva Lace
Belly: White Bucktail
Back: Pink Bucktail with Silver Mylar Strips
Stripe: Grizzly Hackle on each side
Overback: Peacock Herl
Head: Pink Lacquer
Eyes: Black on White Lacquer
Plate #6, Fly #6

PINK CHIRONOMID

Hook: Tiemco 2487. Size 16-20
Body: Flo. Pink (#06) Larva Lace Body Material.
(slipover method)
Collar: Light Hare's Ear
Plate #13, Fly #10

PINK EGG

Hook: Mustad 9523.
Body: Pink Poly Yarn
Inner Egg: Hot Pink Poly Yarn
Thread: Nylon Translucent
Plate #8, Fly #13

PINK KRYSTAL BULLET

Hook: Mustad 36890. Size 4-8.
Thread: Hot Pink
Underbody: Open Cell Foam
Body: Flour. Pink (#06) Larva Lace Body
Material
Tail: Pink Krystal Flash
Head: Pink Krystal Flash
Wing: Pink Krystal Flash
Plate #8, Fly #5

PINK MARABOU FLASH – TARPON FLY

Hook: Mustad 34007. Size 1/0
Inner Tail: Fluorescent Pink Marabou
Back: Fluorescent Pink Marabou mixed with
crystal fibers
Hackle: Fluorescent Red Saddle Hackle
Head: Fluorescent Red Thread, lacquer heavy
Plate #5, Fly #5

PINK SHRIMP

Hook: Mustad 37160
Body: Fl. Pink (#06) Larva Lace Body Material
Beard: Pink dyed Grizzly Fibers]
Legs: Pink Ostrich
Thread: Nylon Translucent
Eyes: Black Permanent Marker
Plate #15, Fly #5

POLAR SHRIMP

Hook: Mustad 36890. Size 4-6.
Tail: Orange and Red Hackle Fibers
Underbody: Red Floss
Body: Clear (#03) Larva Lace Body Material
Hackle: Red and Orange Saddle

Wing: White Calf Tail
Thread: Black
Plate #8, Fly #12

POLY BACK SHRIMP – Grey

Hook: TMC 2487
Body: Grey Synthetic Dubbing
Back: Poly Bag Strip
Rib: Nylon Translucent Thread
Head: Black Permanent Marker
Plate #15, Fly #12

POLY BACK SHRIMP

Hook: Tiemco 2487. Size 16.
Body: Orange/yellow synthetic dubbing
Back: Poly Bag Strip
Rib: Nylon Translucent Thread
Plate #15, Fly #9

POLY HUMPY

Hook: Mustad 94840. Size 12-18
Body: Pale Yellow Floss
Tail: Brown Hackle Fibers
Back: Light Tan Synthetic Dubbing
Wings: Light Tan Synthetic Dubbing
Hackle: Brown – Same as Tail
Plate #14, Fly #4

PURPLE SKUNK

Hook: Mustad 36890. Size 4-6
Tail: Purple Hackle Fibers
Underbody: Purple Floss
Overbody: Clear (#03) Larva Lace Body Material
Hackle: Purple Saddle
Wing: White Calf Tail
Thread: Black
Plate #8, Fly #9

RAINBOW TROUT

Hook: Mustad 79580 or 94720. Size 6-12
Underbody: Larva Lace Fly Tying Foam –White
(Wet)
Side Stripe: Flor. Red (#06) Larva Lace Body
Material
Dots: Black indelible ink
Underback: Swiss straw (Olive)
Overbody: Clear (#03) Larva Lace Body Material
Overback: Olive Marabou under Black Marabou
Head: Black 4/0 Uni-thread
Eye: White vinyl paint with black dot

RED ANT

Hook: Mustad 94840. Size 14-18.
Body: Red Closed Cell Foam
Hackle: Red
Thread: Red 8/0 Uni-thread
Plate #14, Fly #17

RED CHIRONOMID

Hook: Tiemco 2487. Size 16-20
Body: Blood Red (#14) Larva Lace
Thread: Nylon Transluscent
Plate #13, Fly #9

RED SAN JUAN WORM

Hook: Mustad 37160. Size 10
Body: Red (#14) Larva Lace Body Material
Thread: 6/0 Red Uni-thread
Plate #13, Fly #7

RIVER WITCH

Hook: Mustad 79580. Size 2-10
Tail: Marabou with crystal hair Rib (same color as back)
Underbody: Larva lace fly tying foam (white) (wet). For buildup cover with pearlescent mylar tinsel
Overbody: Larva lace body material – half hitch weave, Top – Colored, Bottom – Clear
Thorax: Colored chenille same as back
Hackle: Saddle hackle same color as chenille
Thread: Same color as hackle
Fluorescent colors are great for Alaskan fishing with this pattern
Plate 10, Fly #6

ROYAL RENEGADE

Hook: Mustad 94840. Size 12-16.
Tab: Gold Tinsel
Back Hackle: Brown
Back Body: Peacock Herl
Center: Red Metallic Tinsel
Front Body: Peacock Herl
Front Hackle: White
Thread: 8/0 Uni-thread
Plate #14, Fly #12

ROYAL SOFT HACKLE

Hook: Tiemco 5262 or Mustad 39060. Size 12-16
Body: Blood Red (#14) Larva Lace Body Material
Rib: Silver Metallic Tinsel
Collar: Peacock Herl
Hackle: Partridge Thread: 8/0 Uni-thread
Plate #16, Fly #1

SAN JUAN WORM

Hook: Mustad 3716. Size 2-6 (Straighten out 50% of Bend)
Body: Tan Ultra Chenille.
Thread: 4/0, Match with color of body
Plate #13, Fly #1

SENIOR CITIZEN

Hook: TMC 5262 or Mustad 79580. Size 4-18
Underbody: Pearl Mylar
Body: Clear (#03) Larva Lace Body Material
Back: Black and Yellow Marabou
Head: Build up with thread
Thread: 3/0 Black or Mono Chord
Plate 9, Fly #2

SHAD FLY

Hook: Mustad 3906B. Size 4-10
Tail: Marabou Flor. Chartreuse
Underbody: Larva Lace fly tying foam
Body: Fluorescent Chartreuse (#04) Larva Lace body material
Eyes: Bead Chain
Thread: Same color as Tail and Body
This pattern also works well in fluorescent orange and red

SILVER BLUE SOFT HACKLE

Hook: TMC 5262; Mustad 39063. Size 10-16
Underbody: Silver Mylar
Body: Clear (#03) Larva Lace Body Material
Wing: Grey/Goose wing
Hackle: Blue Dun Hen
Thread: Grey 8/0 Uni-thread
Plate 16, Fly #2

SKUNK

Hook: Mustad 36890. Size 4-6
Tail: Red Hackle Fibers
Body: Black (#01) Larva Lace Body Material
Hackle: Black Saddle Hackle
Wing: White Calf Tail
Thread: Black
Plate #8, Fly #8

SOFT BACK STONE

Hook: Mustad 79580. Size 8-10.
Tail: Javilina
Abdomen: Black Rabbit
Underbody: Open Cell Foam
Body: Black (#01) Larva Lace Body Material
Back: Turkey Feather (tail)
Thorax: Black Rabbit Dubbing
Wing Case: Fake Fern
Ribbing: Nylon Thread
Thread: Black
Plate #10, Fly #5

SPARKLE CADDIS EMERGER – Grey

Hook: Tiemco 2487 or Daiichi 1150. Size 14-16
Body: Grey (#08) Larva Lace Body Material
Rib: Nylon Translucent Thread
Bubbles: Antron
Collar: Antron mixed Dubbing
Legs: Hackle Fibers
Plate #16, Fly #10

SPARKLE DUNK CHARLIE

Hook: Mustad 34007. Size 4-6
Tail: White Calf Tail
Underbody: White Open Cell Foam with Glitter Pen spread over the foam surface
Underbody Coating: While Glitter Pen is still wet, dunk in extra fine Pearl Glitter.
Thread: Larva Lace Translucent
Eyes: Chrome Bead Chain
Body: Clear (#03) Larva Lace Body Material
Back: White Calf Tail with a mix of crystal fibers
Plate #8, Fly #4

SPARKLE NYMPH

Hook: Tiemco 5262 or Mustad 3906B. Size 16-18
Tail: Brown Hackle Fibers
Underbody: Pearl Crystal Hair
Body: Nylon Translucent Thread Overwrap
Thorax: Hare's Ear
Wing Case: Pheasant Tail
Legs: Pheasant Tail
Plate #16, Fly #8

SPARKLE SHRIMP (PINK)

Hook: Mustad 36890. Size 2-6. Thread: Same color as body
Shell Back and Tail: Pearl Flashabou (same piece)
Body: Chenille
Hackle: Same color as body
Plate #7, Fly #7

SPARKLE SHRIMP (CHARTREUSE)

Hook: Mustad 36890. Size 2-6
Thread: Same color as body
Shell Back and Tail: Pearl Flashabou (same piece)
Body Chenille
Hackle: Same color as body
Plate #7, Fly #8

SPARKLE WOOLY BUGGER

Hook: Mustad 79580. Size 4-10
Tail: Black Marabou
Body: Green Sparkle Yarn
Hackle: Black Saddle
Thread: Black
Plate #9, Fly #3

STINGER

Hook: Mustad 34007. Size 4-8
Underbody: Red and Pink Floss
Body: Clear (#03) Larva Lace Body Material
Eyes: Small Lead Eyes
Thread: Danville Yellow
Plate #12, Fly #4

SURF CANDY (Popovics)

Hook: Mustad 34007. Size 1/0
Tail: Badger Hackle with stem clipped
Inner body: Silver Mylar Tubing
Outer body: Ultra Hair
Head: Epoxy
Gill: Red Permanent Marker
Eyes: Prism Tape Eyes
Plate #6, Fly #1

SYNTHETIC MICKEY FINN

Hook: Mustad 79580. Size 6-12
Underbody: Silver Mylar Tinsel
Overbody: Clear (#03) Larva Lace Body Material (overwrap)
Wing: Yellow and Red Fishair
Thread: Black
Plate #9, Fly #1

TAN BEND BACK

Hook: Mustad 9353 ST.
Body: Silver Mylar
Body Overwrap: Clear (#03) Larva Lace Body Material
Belly: Tan Bucktail
Back: Tan Bucktail with Silver Mylar Strips
Stripe: Grizzly Hackle on each side
Over-back: Peacock Herl
Head: Pink Lacquer
Eyes: Black on White Lacquer
Plate #6, Fly #8

TAN MADAM X

Hook: Mustad 94840. Size 12-14
Body: Pearl Crystal Hair
Tail: Deer Hair
Leg: White Elastic Strands
Head: Deer Hair
Thread: Tan 8/0 Uni-thread
Plate #14, Fly #13

TAN SHRIMP

Hook: Mustad 37160 or Eagle Claw 141. Size 14-16
Body: Shrimp Color (#12) Body Material
Beard: Grizzly Fibers
Legs: Tan Ostrich
Thread: Nylon Translucent
Eyes: Black Permanent Marker
Plate #15, Fly #3

TOOTIE FRUITIE

Hook: Mustad 3906B. Size 8-12
* **Tail:** Elastic Strip
Underbody: Larva Lace Open Cell Foam
Body: Larva Lace Body Material for Back and Belly (Half Hitch Weave Method)
** **Hackle:** Dyed Grizzly (Same color as belly)
Thorax: Black Chenille
Thread: 4/0 Black Uni-thread
* Color same as belly underbody of fly
** Popular belly colors Flor. Orange, Flor. Chartreuse, Yellow, Brown, Olive

TRICO SPINNER – (Tricoythodes)

Hook: Mustad 94840. Size 18-20.
Tail: Fib-Betts (black)
Body: Black Thin Strip Closed Cell Foam
Wings: White Thin Strip Closed Cell Foam

Thorax: Black Dubbed Seal-X
Thread: Black 8/0 Uni-thread
Plate # 14, Fly #16

WATER BEETLE – Wet

Hook: Mustad 3906B. Size 10-14
Underbody: Blue Larva Lace fly tying foam (wet)
Body: Black (#01) Larva Lace body material Half Hitch (weave method)
Belly: Olive (#09) Larva Lace body material
Collar: Black dubbed rabbit
Throat: Black soft hackle fiber
Thread: 3/0 black Uni-thread

WHITEFISH FLY

Hook: Mustad 3906B. Size 12-16
Body: Orange (#10) Larva Lace Body Material
Hackle: Partridge
Thread: Black
Plate #16, Fly #4

WOVEN DAMSEL

Hook: Tiemco TMC 200. Size 8-10.
Tail: Olive Marabou
Body: Olive (#09) Larva Lace Body Material (half-hitch weave method)
Thorax: Hare's Ear
Hackle: Olive Saddle
Wing Case: Turkey Tail
Eyes: Burnt Yellow (#13) Larva Lace Body Material
Thread: Olive
Plate #10 Fly #2

WOVEN STONE

Hook: Mustad 79580. Size 4X (Apply slight bend)
Abdomen: Dark Brown Beaver Dubbing
Tail: Brown Biot
Body: Brown (#02) Larva Lace Body Material
Thorax: Dark Brown Rabbit
Wing Case: Burnt Pheasant Feather
Antenna: Brown Biot
Head: Dark Brown Beaver Dubbing
Plate #10, Fly #3

YELLOW GRIZZLY TARPON FLY

Hook: Mustad 34007. Size 3/0
Tail: Yellow Calf Tail
Inner Wing: Yellow-dyed Grizzly Saddle

Outer Wing: Yellow-dyed Grizzly Saddle
Hackle: Yellow-dyed Grizzly Saddle
Thread: Yellow
Eyes: Black on White Vinyl Paint
Plate #5, Fly #3

YELLOW HALFBACK CHARLIE
Hook: Mustad 34007. Size 4-8
Tail: Golden Pheasant Crest
Body: Yellow (#13) Larva Lace Body Material
Underweave: White Open Cell Foam
Eyes: Chrome Bead Chain

Thread: Nylon Translucent
Plate #12, Fly #2

ZONKER
Hook: Mustad 9672. Size 4-8.
Tail: Unraveled Mylar Tubing
Underbody: Lead Tape
Body: Silver Mylar Tubing
Back: Rabbit Strip
Hackle: Grizzly
Thread: Black
Plate #9, Fly #10

Fly
Patterns

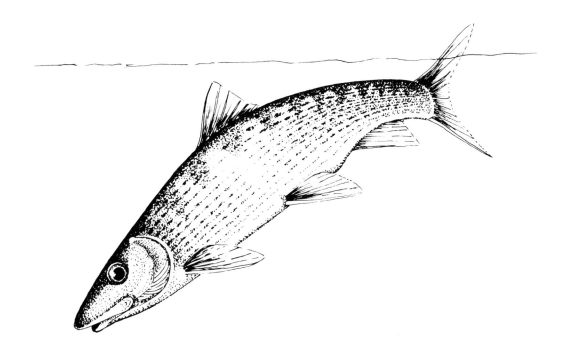

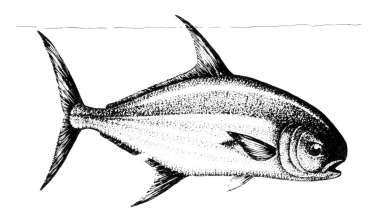

SALT WATER PATTERNS

CAMERA'S CRAB

A few years ago a small Deer Hair Permit Crab appeared on our fly shop shelves and in our fly fishing periodicals. This fly gained rapid popularity among Permit fly fishermen.

Being a newcomer to salt water fly fishing and a tyer with less than perfect hair spinning ability, I had the need to tie a Permit Crab, but by a technique other than the existing pattern. After putting a lot of thought and trial tying into this critter, I decided I liked the wool body better than the deer hair because of its water absorbtion qualities. Changing the legs and the weight system to meet my needs, I felt that this was the crab I was looking for.

CAMERA'S CRAB (hard claw) Plate #11, Fly #1

Materials:

Hook: Mustad 34007. Size 1/0-4

Thread: Larva Lace Translucent (Fine)

Body: Dubbed Wool (Spun)-Light Sand Color or Dark Grey

Claw: Pheasant Back Feather (Rooster)

Legs: Shrimp Color (#12) Larva Lace Body Material

Inner Legs: Orange Crystal Hair

Eyes: Lead

Step 1. Tie in pre-made pheasant feather claw.

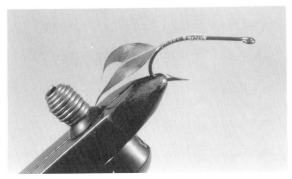

Step 2. Tie in Lead Eyes.

Step 3. Dub on Wool using a dubbing loop. After each bunch is spun on, pack in very tightly.

Step 4. Clip off wool so you are down to where the wool is very tight.

Step 5. Continue snipping wool until you have completed the length of the body.

Step 6. Clip the wool until entire top is down to a hard mat surface. (Do not clip sides yet.)

Step 7. Turn crab upside down in the vise.

Step 8. Clip the remaining wool on the top side leaving only the wool sticking out from the sides.

Step 9. Trim sides to a round or oval shape.

Step 10. Prepare Larva Lace legs by inserting orange crystal hair into shrimp color body material. Then cut into 2″ pieces.

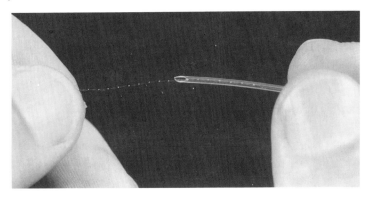

Step 11. Tie a tight overhand knot approximately ¹/₂″ from the end of each piece of larva lace. This will retain the crystal hair and give a leg joint appearance.

Step 12. Turn crab back to the position in the vise as when started.

Step 13. The surface that is top-side is the belly of the crab. Put a light coat of hot glue on the entire belly surface.

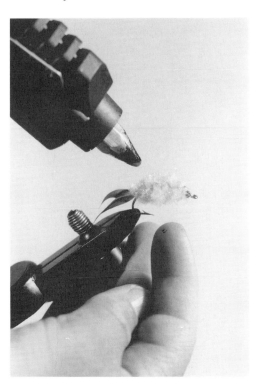

Step 14. Place legs on one at a time. Each leg will have a bend in it. Place the leg on the crab with the bend and short end facing straight up. When the crab is completed and turned right side up you will see that the legs will then look natural. Apply a drop of hot glue to each leg when setting it in position. Camera's Crab has two legs on each side.

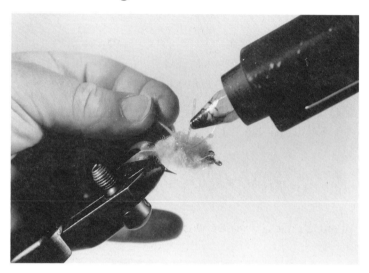

Step 15. Using the tip of the hot glue gun, heat up the body glue and apply a little more if necessary.

Step 16. While hot glue is warm and workable, take the crab from the vise and place it on a smooth glass surface. Apply pressure straight down putting the crab in the exact position you want him to take when sitting under water.

    The glue will harden up in about one minute, then you can peel the crab up.

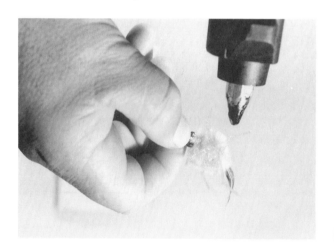
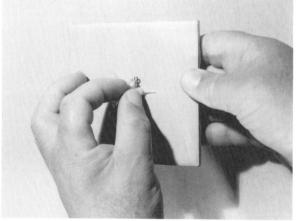

Step 17. Trim away any excess glue that may have squeeze out from the sides.

Step 18. Apply shaded lines or dots on the Crabs back with darker shade Pantone Pens if crabs in your area have a special shell design. The flat hot glue section can also be painted or colored to represent your local critters.

SOFT CLAW CAMERA'S CRAB - Plate #11, Fly #3

Step 1. Tie in Calf Tail

Step 2. Tie in small grizzly hackle tips.

Pick up at Step 3. on above pattern.

Variations of the Camera's Crab are in the body materials, legs, and adhesives. Many crabs you'll see have been tied with spun deer hair instead of wool and the legs are elastic bands.

Deer hair works very well because of the color variation that you can tie in. When tying a deer hair crab you will want to place some coiled lead on the belly before you put on the legs. I have found that hot glue works best for me, however, many tyers use white silicone caulking (the same type used when trimming the bathroom tub). This silicone adhesive gives the tyer a little more working time.

I feel the Larva Lace legs are far superior to the elastic bands because the hot sun quickly destroys the rubber legs while the vinyl remains unaffected.

STREAMERS

The streamer is a fly that imitates a small minnow and is usually attacked by its prey with great vigor. These flys are tied relatively sparsely to give the slim appearance of young fry. One of the most popular is the Bucktail Streamer. The bucktail streamer obtained its name because of the material originally used to shade its upper body and back. The bottom was usually flat silver or gold tinsel wrapped around the hook shank to represent the bright belly of the minnow.

As synthetics came about the streamer (or bucktail) was one of the flys that was always used as a test for new materials. As good as deer tail is, it is very fragile and will break after a few fish have been caught. Many of the metal tinsels have now been substituted with flat mylar which can fray after exposure to the rakers of a few trout. The following tips and techniques will show you how to tie an all synthetic streamer which will be just as effective as the early pattern but far more durable.

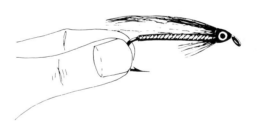

Streamer Fly

Tips when Tying Streamers:

1. Painted eyes will always brighten up your flies but I find them more practical from sizes eight and larger. (see Painting Eyes, page 109.)

2. Tie your streamers according to the size fry you are imitating.

3. When wrapping over thin Mylar with vinyl it sometimes helps to put light coat of head cement over the Mylar and let it dry. This will prevent the Mylar from distorting when being overwrapped.

4. Make sure you always tie in the vinyl first and from the front of the hook to the back. This will assure an even body.

5. If weighting your streamer with lead, keep the lead just forward of the middle of the hook shank.

6. If you intend to have a Mylar body over lead you should wrap a layer of open cell foam over the lead to assure a smooth and tapered surface. Then wrap the Mylar over the foam.

7. When using Mylar Tinsel as a ribbing material it is now available as gold on one side and silver on the other. When applying this type of Mylar to your fly the rib color should be tied face down.

Synthetic Hair Substitutes for Streamers

*Ultra Hair-by JH Thompson
*Fishair-by Fish Hair Products
*Fish Fuzz-by Gehrke Products
*Streamer Hair-by Wapsi

STREAMER PATTERNS

SQUIRREL TAIL

Materials:
Hook: Mustad 79580
Thread: Black
Underbody: Silver Flat Mylar
Overbody: Clear (#03) Larva Lace Body Material
Wing: Gray Squirrel Tail
Throat: Red Hackle Fibers

SENIOR CITIZEN – Plate #9, Fly #2
Materials:
Hook: Mustad-79580
Thread: Black
Underbody: Flat Pearl Mylar
Overbody: Clear (#03) Larva Lace Body Material
Wing: Yellow over Black Marabou (smaller amount of yellow than black)
Eye: optional, Black on White Paint

BLACK NOSE DACE
Materials:
Hook: Mustad 79580
Thread: Black
Tag: Bright Red Yard (very short)
Underbody: Flat Silver Mylar
Overbody: Clear (#03) Larva Lace Body Material
Wing: White Bucktail on the Bottom, Black Bucktail in the middle, natural Brown Bucktail on the Top.

MICKEY PEARL
Materials: Same as Mickey Finn but with pearl body
Hook: Mustad 79580
Thread: Black
Underbody: Flat Pearl Mylar
Overbody: Clear (#03) Larva Lace Body Material
Wing: Small amount of yellow bucktail over the hook with a small patch of red bucktail on top. Then top the red bucktail with larger amounts of yellow

SEQUINS STREAMER (G-STRING)

The Sequins Streamer is a fly that you will find difficult locating in any other book other than the cover page of Duncan's Alaskan Adventures catalog. This pattern was designed by myself and Don Puterbaugh while fishing for Silver Salmon on the Italia River near Yakatat, Alaska.

This particular year we had extreme low water conditions and were confronting the fish in 1 to 3 feet of water. Fishing near the mouth of the river still in the tidal zone, these fish had not yet abandoned their feeding instincts. The sequins sided streamer appears as a natural food source as well as an attractor and has proven itself to be a very effective Coho salmon pattern.

SEQUINS STREAMER (G-string)

Materials:

Hook: Mustad 79580. Size 2 & 4

Thread: 4/0

Underbody: Open Cell Foam

Body: Laced Sequins (Silver)

Underwing: White Streamer Hair

Overwing: Purple, Chartreuse, Orange or Green Streamer Hair

Weight: LED (Flat Lead)

Step 1. Wrap on approximately $3/4$ of an inch of flat lead (LED) to the hook shank.

Step 2. Attach tying thread and secure the LED

Step 3. Tie in a strip of open cell foam, and form a tapered streamer body.

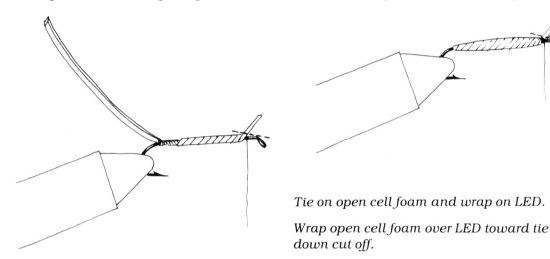

Tie on open cell foam and wrap on LED.

Wrap open cell foam over LED toward tie down cut off.

Step 4. Tie on a piece of sequins attaching it by the eye of the hook. When attaching this material, tie in by the center cord.

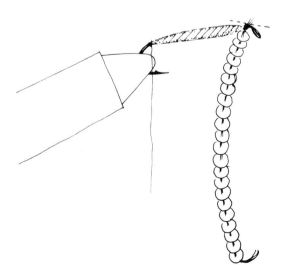

Tie on string sequins, length a little over twice hook length, then knot and cut tying thread. Reattach tying thread at rear of hook as illustrated.

Step 5. Pull sequins back along the side of the streamer and secure by the bend of the hook.

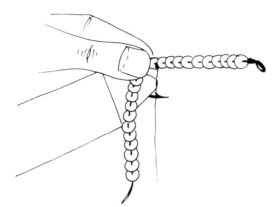

With tying thread, tie down sequins strand between sequins onto connecting sequins thread, while keeping sequins strand taunt with left hand.

Step 6. Bring sequins back along the far side of the hook and secure one eye width back from the eye. When bringing thread forward wrap thread between each sequins scale, hiding the thread.

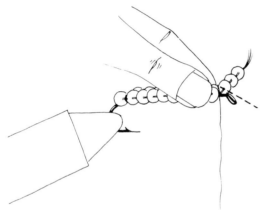

After tying down sequins strand, knot tying thread and cut. Retie tying thread at front of hook as illustrated. Pull sequins strand forward on opposite side of hook. While keeping tight, tie down sequin strand. Cut off sequin strand.

Step 7. Attach underwing

Step 8. Attach overwing and form head with tying thread.

Step 9. Apply head cement and paint on eyes if desired.

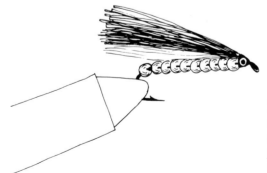

Tie on white under wing, then flourescent chartreuse, orange or pink wing. Then tie on approximately one dozen strands of Flashabou, gold, silver or pearl. Finish head and knot and cut tying thread.

FENDER FLIES

by Robert Ransom

Although I first began experimenting with mylar as a fly material in the early 1980s, it has been during the last few years that the majority of the Fender concept has been resolved. This fly was inspired by the Japanese technique of folding shaped, dried fish skin patterns over hook shanks to make small bait imitations, the use of protective sheaths on off-shore trolling feathers and Dave Whitlock's use of self-adhesive mylar in his prismatic minnow. It's designed for the salt water but is applicable for fresh water in smaller sizes.

It was named the Fender Fly because it provides a metallic-appearing protection for the fragile base of wings and tails. This system also makes a good impression of baitfish profiles or gill plates and a good background upon which to render eyes.

The unique qualities of the system as are:

1. The way the self-adhesive mylar is reinforced with strapping tape.

2. The way the eye is constructed by using shirt snaps as rivets and the way these rivets are filled with pigmented epoxy to make the eyes.

3. The way the face patterns are cut to produce impressions of baitfish flank and gill plate silhouettes

4. The way cement is utilized to bond the snap eyes through the fly dressing, producing a more durable fly. (The glue penetrates the dressing under the Fender face so that the back of the snaps are glued together.)

Although the full testing of this fly is still in its infancy, the list of responsive quarry is growing: in Baja California: Yellowfin and Skipjack tunas, Dorado (Dolphin fish or Mahi Mahi), Needlefish, Yellowtail and Sierra fell for the Fenders. In Texas: Largemouth Bass and Redfish joined the club. Salmon have eaten the fly in Alaska. Trout and Bonito did the same in California. The North-East coast produced Lingcod and Rockfish. Cotuit, Massachusetts contributed a Bluefish, Canada Steelhead. The most recent additions are Venezuela's Pavon or Peacock Bass, Payara and the infamous Piranha.

This system is applicable to many patterns or pattern categories. Some of these that are particularly suited to the Fender face are:

Fur Strips	Bucktails
Lefty's Deceivers	Matukas
Marabou Matukas	Streamers
Nelson's Aztec	

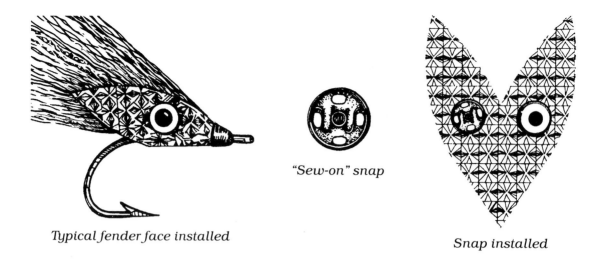

Typical fender face installed

"Sew-on" snap

Snap installed

TYING FENDER FLIES

Hook: Mustad 3407, 34011, 9175; Eagle Claw #254; Partridge BJSSF,S6
(Homassa Special) Or any heavy wire, large gap, generous eyed hook

Thread: Monocord "A", Danville Flat-waxed Nylon, Danville Plus

Tail/wing: Bucktail, Saddle Hackle, Nylon (Fish Hair and similar), Flashabou or Krystal flash, Long dense fur strip (Fox)

Body: Diamond Braid (selected patterns)

Fender Face: Prismatic Mylar or equiv. reinforced with fiberglass strapping tape, Alternately 10 mil Clear or Colored Vinyl

Eye: 4/0 to 2/0 Dritz sew-on shirt snaps filled with Quick Set Epoxy
pigmented with Opaque Resin Color

Size: #2 to 5/0

Glue: Thin Cyanoacrylate, such as "Zap" Quick-Set Epoxy, Clear, thick
head cement such as "rice's" or the decoupage coating "Joli-Glaze"

Making the Fender Face

1. Cut a 1″ strip from the roll of 1 1/2″ wide fiber-reinforced strapping tape. Stick
about 1/4″ of this to the end of the tape remaining on the roll sticky side to
sticky side. Pull 8 to 10″ of the tape from the roll and use the little tab on the
end to attack the longer strip to a cutting surface so that it is sticky side up.
Cut the longer strip from the roll and use another small tab of tape to stretch
it flat holding it down against the cutting board. The best cutting surface is
plastic or glass.

2. Cut a strip of self-adhesive mylar 1³/₄″ wide equal in length to the strapping tape. Remove the protective backing. Align the mylar over the tape by holding its ends and allowing the center to hang so that it will touch first. Gradually lower the ends, sticking the tape and mylar together. The mylar should extend in width about ¹/₈″ beyond the tape and equal it in length. Press the two together insuring a good bond.

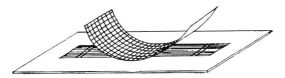

3. Cut the tape tabs off and remove the laminated mylar. Fold the material in half on the long axis of the tape. The sticky back of the excess mylar will hold the material in a folded position. Put the face material aside.

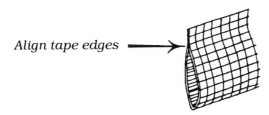

Align tape edges ➡

4. Choose a face pattern. Cut it out to make a paper template. Make sure the seams stay aligned.

5. Fold it over the laminated mylar making sure the seams are aligned. Cut out a face following the template. (Sharp serrated scissors such as Thompsons' or Kershaw Skeeters work best.)

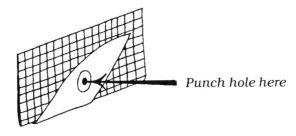

Punch hole here

6. Make a hole where the center of the eye will be. Although a bodkin makes an adequate hole for the smallest size snaps, a ¹/₁₆″ leather punch works best.

7. Repeat the process producing 6 to 8 faces. Actually, it is best to make 5 or 6 dozen or more faces at a time before installing them.

8. To make the eyes use Dritz "sew on" snaps from a fabric store in the appropriate size for the fly. The snaps come in diameters from ³/₁₆″ to ⁹/₁₆″. The ³/₁₆″ size is called 3/0, ⁹/₃₂″ is 2/0, ⁵/₁₆″ is 1/0, ³/₈″ is size 1, ⁹/₁₆″ is size 3. The most useful seem to be 4/0, 3/0, 2/0. They are nickel-plated or black,

painted brass and are rust proof. (Note:the 3/0 eye size is not carried by every fabric store.) Insert the male half of the snap through the prepared hole in the face from the tape side to the mylar side as shown.Snap the female half onto the male. Repeat for the other eye.

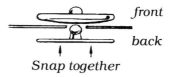

front

back

Snap together

9. Place the face with both eyes assembled down on a firm surface like a hunk of flat metal and gently peen the two sides of the snap together with a sharp tap on the front side with a hammer. This makes the snap into a rivet.

Hit here

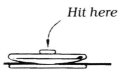

10. Prepare a holder for the faces by attaching a strip of double-face tape to a piece of cardboard. Stick the back of the faces down to this strip to hold them flat for filling.

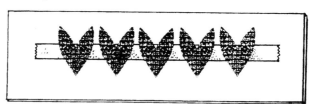

11. Mix a small amount of clear 5-minute epoxy on a piece ofcardboard. Pick up a drop of the cement on the end of a small dowel ($^3/_{16}''$ is a good size). Dab the drop into the cupped surface of the female snap-side. This should only fill the snap to the level shown. Repeat the process for the balance of the eyes prepared. This will prevent pigmented epoxy from leaking under the snap.

Clear level

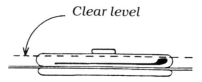

12. Prepare a cardboard palette of resin dye. The brand I've been using is called Opaque Resin Color (concentrated) manufactured by Gerisch Products Inc. of Torrance, California. A pencil eraser size of each color is fine. I most often use white or yellow eyes with black pupils.

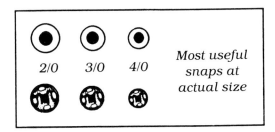

Most useful snaps at actual size

2/0   3/0   4/0

13. Mix a silver dollar size puddle of epoxy with about a matchheads worth of the lighter pigment. It's important to be sparing with the pigment as it may retard setting.

14. Take the small dowel and barely dip it into the puddle of light epoxy. By keeping the dowel turning, the amount of epoxy may be controlled. Then take the drop and dab it over the snap, making a shallow puddle. When lifting the dowel from the puddle, rotate it with a little "Dairy Queen Twist".This will keep the epoxy in snap.

15. Repeat the process with dark epoxy for the smaller diameter pupil. Use a smaller dot than the ultimate pupil size as it will spread slightly before curing. Do this on a horizontal surface and keep it that way until the epoxy is well set.

    It's best to let the eyes cure for a day or two to eliminate stickiness.

Filled snap

FENDER INSTALLATION INSTRUCTIONS

1. For the Fender face to sit well on the fly, a tapered thread-covered base between $1/8''$ and $3/16''$ diameter and $3/16''$ to $5/16''$ long is needed behind the eye (size number 2 and up). Make a thread base approximately the angle of the finished Fender face.

2. Apply a penetrating cement such as cyanoacrylate or almost any thinned head cement to the thread wraps. Then work Bond 527 multipurpose cement into the dressing where the face will ultimately cover it. The Bond 527 must connect the backs of the two snap eyes together by penetrating the wing from one eye to the other.

3. When installing hackles on a side-saddled fly, use a little 527 to help mount them in with thread. Then add a little to the outside of the feather to help attach the face.

4. Before the cement is dry, apply a coating to the back of the Fender face covering the snaps and mount the face by placing it slightly forward of its ultimate position and sliding it up where it belongs.

5. For ultimate durability, attach the face without Bond 527 and cement the eye area together by carefully folding the face back and inserting 5-minute epoxy into the dressing behind the eye. (See instructions for Fender-Faced Hi-tie.)

6. Top installation (mounting the face with the seam above the winging):

   A. Start attaching the Fender with the thread about $3/16''$ away from the eye. While holding the Fender with the vise hand, wrap forward toward the hook eye. Make sure the first wrap binds the bottom of the near side of the Fender under the hook shank, flat to the thread base.
   B. Make a narrow band of five of six firm initial wraps to attach the face.
   C. While holding the wraps stable with thumb and forefinger of the vise hand, move the thread directly behind the eye.
   D. Build a dam of another six or eight wraps to stop the thread from sliding forward while wrapping back toward the attachment point.
   E. Make the thread head in two or three firm layers and whip-finish.

7. Bottom installation (mounting the face with the seam against the hook shank, folding the face up and over the winning):

   A. Simply wrap back from a point directly behind the eye, building a $3/16''$ to $1/4''$ head of adjacent wraps.
   B. Return wrap, whip finishing to the hook eye.

8. Place the fly under a magazine to help keep it flat until the Bond 527 is dry or the epoxy is set.

9. After the interior glue sets apply a drop or two of thin CA glue to the exterior wraps for maximum penetration.

10. Use the plastic decoupage coating "Joli-Glaze" as the final cement. Coating diamond braid mylar bodies and dropping a little of this cement into the cavity under the top installed Fender helps increase durability.

FENDER-FACED NYLON HI-TIE

This pattern is a variation on the Hi- Tie made popular by Mark Sosin. The high front wing angle and minimum bulk at the hook shank make perfect for receiving a Fender face. Tying the Hi- Tie with slippery materials such as Fish Hairs Fly Tying or Nylon Lure Dressing can produce a super strong fly particularly when the bunches of the hair are tied in at their middle to avoid pull-out.

1. Hold the face up to the hook in its ultimate location as shown. (Not the point where the hook shank first projects from the rear face.) Tie in the thread near the eye and wrap back just short of this point.

2. Make a small lump of 6 to 10 thread wraps and cement with a drop of CA glue. This will kick the tail up to blend with the winging.

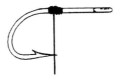

3. Select a bunch of dressing about $1/16''$ in diameter and a little more than twice the ultimate length of the wing. Tie it in on top the hook at the center of the bunch. Wrap forward about six turns wrap back about three turns. Pull the forward half of the bunch back over the wraps. Bind down, keeping the bunches stacked on top of each other. Wrap forward bringing thread just in front of the fold.

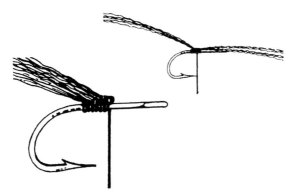

4. Tie in the next bunch here as above. Continue to repeat the process, moving up the eye. Crystal Hair may be folded in with the dressing for flash.

5. The last bunch should fold tight to the beginning of the hookeye. Bring the thread back in close wraps forward to this point after binding down the last half of the last bunch. Let the bobbin hang.

6. The best Fender faces to use with this pattern are bottom mounted by folding them with the seam against the hook shank, up and over the wing. Hold the face temporarily in position with the vise hand while pulling upon the thread with the bobbin to keep it out of the way. Slide the face forward to a point where the front face-taper will wrap around more than $1/2$ the thread head. Remove the face and trim the excess face front.

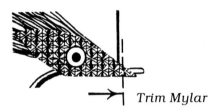

Trim Mylar

7. Carefully apply a penetrating cement such as cyanoacrylate or almost any thinned head cement to the thread wraps. Do not allow the cement to move up the wing with capillary action. Keep the glue down on the thread through sparing use. Before the CA glue sets, slide the face into position with the thread up as before. Make sure the face is in the same plane as the hook. Be careful. Too much CA glue can make its way between your fingers and the fly making it part of your hand!

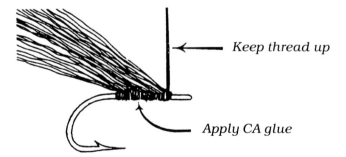

Keep thread up

Apply CA glue

8. While holding the Fender with the vise hand, build a dam of a few wraps just behind the eye to stop the thread from sliding forward. Wrap back $3/16$ to $1/4''$. Make the thread head in two or three firm layers and whip-finish.

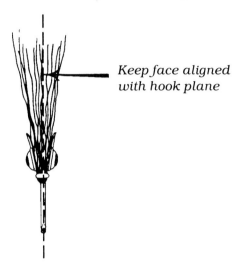

Keep face aligned with hook plane

9. Cement the eye area together by carefully folding the face back, one side at a time, and inserting 5-minute epoxy into the dressing behind the eye. Put a little epoxy on the back of the eye itself before folding it back. Place the fly under a magazine to help keep it flat until the epoxy is set (about 5 minutes).

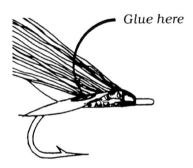

Glue here

10. Apply a drop of CA glue to the wraps.

11. After the CA glues sets. Use a thick water resistant head cement such as the decoupage coating "Joli-Glaze" as the final cement.

BUCKTAIL FENDERS

1. The best bucktail tying methods to use is, again, Sosin's Hi-Tie style. After choosing the face shape and hook you want, hold the face up to the hook in its ultimate location.Note the point were the hook shank first projects from the rear of the face. This is where your first bunch of bucktail will be tied.

2. Tie in the thread near the eye and wrap back just short of this point.

3. Select a bunch of straight bucktail about ¹/₈″ to ³/₁₆″ in diameter. Comb out the short hairs from the butts and even the tips. Use a stacker if you prefer. Measure the hair against the hook shank with the vise hand. The bunch should be about two times the length of the entire hook.

4. Trim the butts and place the hair on top the hook shank so that they project only ³/₁₆″ beyond the hanging thread. Bind the hair down while holding it so that it stays on top the hook-shank. Wrap forward covering the butts.

5. Prepare another bunch of hair equal to the first in diameter.Measure this bunch against the first. For longer shanked hooks a crested effect is produced by using hair bunches of all the same length. For shorter shanked hooks a fan-like effect is produced by making each successive bunch longer than the previous one by the amount used to tie it in (about ³/₁₆″).

6. Flash can be added by catching a few strands of Crystal Hair or Flashabou at their middle with the flared tail butts just before covering them with thread. Trim the strands equal to or a little shorter than the bucktail.

7. Continue tying in bunches right up to the hook eye. At this point, especially with faces mounted on top the hook shank,it may be necessary to tie the last hair bunch in two parts.Tie in the first as above.

8. Tie in the second by stacking it in on top the previous bunch.Trim the butts at a slight angle. The head should have a taper approximating the angle of the finished face. Saddlehackle may be added to each side at this point. Set the saddle so that it divides the bucktail winging evenly top and bottom.

Fender Face Patterns

See diagrams on following three pages.

These shapes are good for shorter style flies. High-tie style bucktails, forward mounted saddle hackle streamers, and synthetic nylon hair streamers work especially well. The round and heart-shaped faces are designed to suggest the gill-plates of baitfish.

Mounting positions for the face patterns listed below shown on Mustad 3407 hooks, size 3/0.

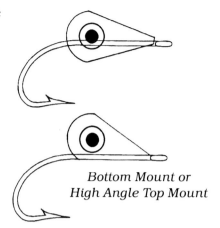

*Bottom Mount or
High Angle Top Mount*

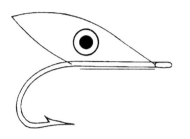 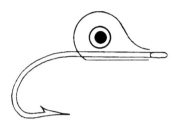

HOOK SIZES	HIGH ANGLE LEAF BOTTOM MOUNT	ROUND BOTTOM MOUNT	HEART	SNAP SIZES
4/0				2/0
3/0				2/0 3/0
2/0				3/0
1/0				4/0
1 & 2				4/0

These leaf-shaped faces are designed to be mounted with their seam on the bottom of the hook shank. They work especially well on flies such as fur strip style streamers, Streakers and Aztecs.

(Mounting positions for the face patterns listed below shown on 3/0 hooks)

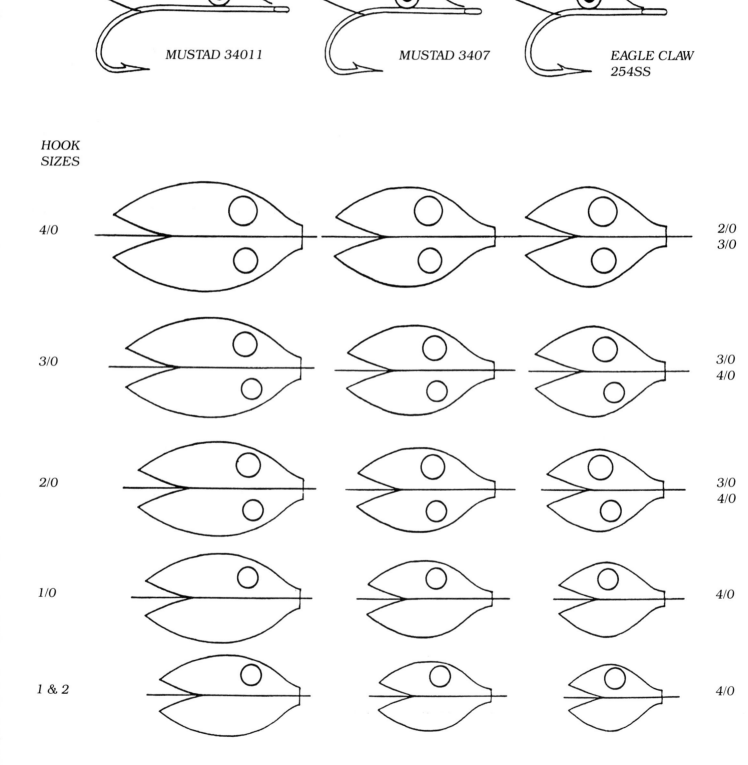

HOOK
SIZES

4/0   2/0
                                                                                                                 3/0

3/0   3/0
                                                                                                                 4/0

2/0   3/0
                                                                                                                 4/0

1/0   4/0

1 & 2   4/0

MUSTAD 34011   MUSTAD 3407   EAGLE CLAW 254SS

Mounting positions for the face patterns listed below
shown on Mustad 3407 hooks size 3/0

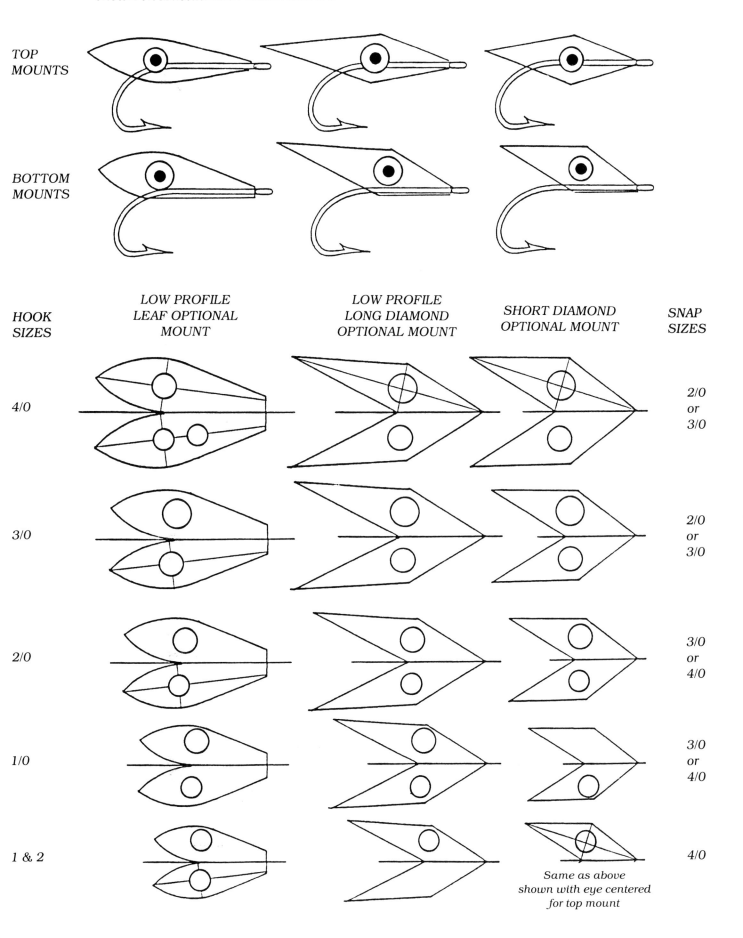

TOP
MOUNTS

BOTTOM
MOUNTS

HOOK SIZES	LOW PROFILE LEAF OPTIONAL MOUNT	LOW PROFILE LONG DIAMOND OPTIONAL MOUNT	SHORT DIAMOND OPTIONAL MOUNT	SNAP SIZES
4/0				2/0 or 3/0
3/0				2/0 or 3/0
2/0				3/0 or 4/0
1/0				3/0 or 4/0
1 & 2				4/0

Same as above
shown with eye centered
for top mount

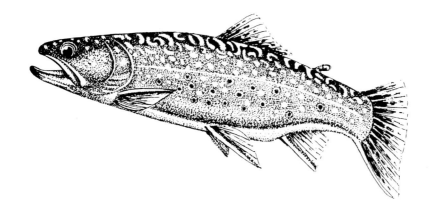

SOFT HACKLED FLYS
WITH SYNTHETICS

The history of the soft hackle fly, according to Sylvester Nemes, author of *The Soft Hackle Fly*, dates back almost 500 years, when Dame Juliana Berners listed 12 flies with the first being a soft hackle named the Donne fly. However, the soft hackle fly has gained very little popularity in the United States. It may be because so much of our fly tying writings have been in the past 20 years and dry flies, nymphs, and steamers seem to have taken the lead in interest. If you invest in Sylvester Nemes' book, you will be pleased with the success you will find in fishing as well as the joy of tying a different series of flies.

As long as the soft hackle fly has been around, it still holds its ground in the age of synthetics. Its simplicity lends itself to all levels of tyers as well as offering compatibility to many new types of body materials. You will find that many of the older patterns call for colored silk floss bodies. When wet, this material has a sheen as well as a translucent appearance. This gives it some of the same qualities as many of the most popular synthetics, but without the durability factor. Special feathers are as important as the synthetics. The following is a list of some of the standard soft hackle feathers used for this type of fly:

Partridge feathers
Grouse hackles
Woodcock hackles
Hen Ring Neck Pheasant
Hen Blue Dun hackle
Grizzly Hen hackle
Cream Badger Hen hackle Sage Hen

A very common pattern in England today is called the pheasant tail. This pattern is one of my favorites because of its high productivity. I tie this pattern from size 12-16, but use a fine gauge copper or gold tinsel instead of the english version using a fine copper wire. I also put on a tab using the same tinsel.

The uniqueness of this pattern is that when the pheasant fibers become frayed, the gold tinsel starts shining through. The longevity of this fly is highly increased.

PHEASANT TAIL SOFT HACKLE — Plate #16, Fly #3

Materials:
Hook: Mustad 3906B. Size 12-16
Tail: 2 to 4 Ring Neck Pheasant Rooster Tail Fibers
Body: Ring Neck Pheasant Rooster Tail and Fine Copper Tinsel
Hackle: Grouse (Brown) Length of Fly Body
Thread: Black Uni-Thread

Step 1. Tie in tinsel along the length of the hook shank.

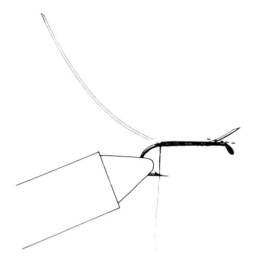

Step 2. Tie in 4 or 5 long pheasant tail fibers.

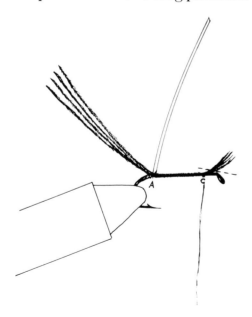

Step 3. Wrap 3 or 4 wraps to make a tab with the tinsel.

Step 4. Wrap pheasant fibers around tinsel then wrap tinsel and fibers forward on hook shank leaving the width of the hook eye for the space needed to tie in your soft hackle.

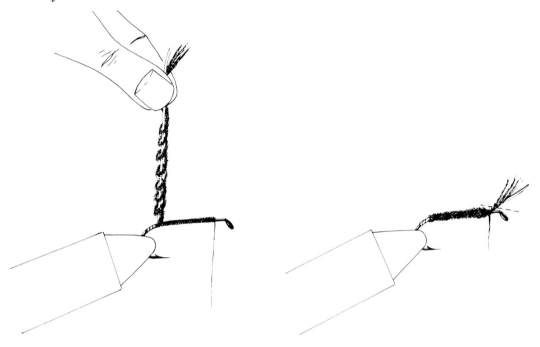

Step 4. Wrap pheasant fibers around tinsel then wrap tinsel and fibers forward on hook shank leaving the width of the hook eye for the space needed to tie in your soft hackle.

Step 5. Pluck desired feather from cape.

Step 6. Pull down fiber so that they are at a 90 degree angle from both sides of the stem.

Step 7. Check for proper fiber length by comparing its length to the body length of the fly. The body of the fly is where the body material starts on the back side of the hook and goes to the front. We do not consider the length of the hook to be the body size, just the wrapped body.

Step 8. Because we seldom wrap the soft hackle more than two turns, we separate the fibers that we are going to use.

Step 9. Tie in fiber stem from the bottom.

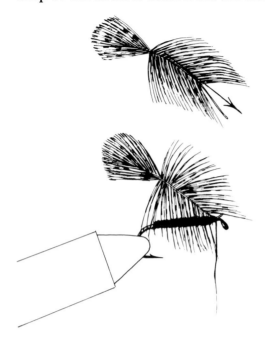

Step 10. Grip hackle from the tip and make 1½ or 2 wraps depending on the amount of fibers desired. This is one time you want to wrap your hackle near the eye of the hook so that when tying off the head of the fly you can over wrap the hackle giving it a swept back effect. These hackle fibers are very susceptible to breaking, so don't pull hard when wrapping.

OTHER SOFT HACKLE PATTERNS

GREEN CADDIS SOFT HACKLE — Plate #16, Fly #6

Materials:
Hook: Mustad 3906 B. Size 14-16
Body: Chartreuse (#04) Larva Lace (slipover technique)
Thread: Larva Lace Translucent, Fine
Collar: Light Hare's Ear
Hackle: Grouse, Grey

SOFT HACKLE WHITE FISH FLY — Plate #16, Fly #4

Materials:
Hook: Size 14-16
Body: Orange (#10) Larva Lace (slipover technique)
Thread: Larva Lace Nylon Translucent, fine
Hackle: Grizzly Hen Hackle

BREAD CRUST NYMPH — Plate #10, Fly #10
(Originally considered a soft hackle fly)

Materials:
Hook: Eagle Claw 141; Mustad 37160. Size 12-16
Underbody: (for larger size) White Open Cell Foam Strip
Rib: Brown Hackle trimmed close to the stem
Collar: Peacock Herl
Hackle: Grouse, Brown

SILVER BLUE SOFT HACKLE — Plate #16, Fly #2

Materials:
Hook: Mustad 3906 B
Underbody: Silver Mylar
Body: Clear (#03) Larva Lace Body Material
Collar: Muskrat, Grey
Hackle: Blue Dun Hen Hackle

ROYAL SOFT HACKLE — Plate #16, Fly #1

Materials:
Hook: Mustad 3906 B
Body: Blood Red (#14) Larva Lace Nymph Rib
Rib: Fine Silver Tinsel
Collar: Peacock Herl
Hackle: Grouse

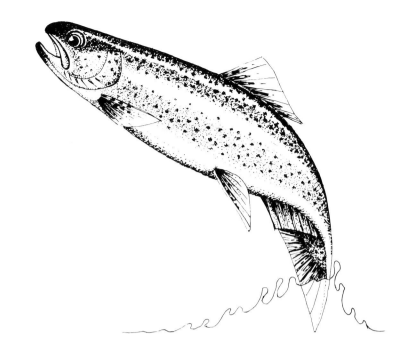

ADULT DAMSEL – MONO

When I asked Larry Walker of Denver, Colorado (a true friend and fellow fly tyer) if he would make a contribution to this book, he popped up with a real winner. This Adult Mono Damsel was originally designed by Gary Borger and Bob Petzel. He wasn't sure of the original recipe, but the following is how he interpreted it. After seeing this pattern on the cover of Gary's new book, *Designing Trout Flies*, I asked him of its origin. Gary proceeded to tell me of the long trial period necessary to develop this pattern into something with which he and Bob were satisfied.

ADULT DAMSEL FLY — Plate #14, Fly #1

Materials:

Hook: Mustad 9671. Size 12 or 14

Thread: Black Mono or Larva Lace Translucent-Dark.

Abdomen: 25 or 30 lb. Braided Mono Dyed Blue. I used Veniard Cambridge Blue Dye.

Wing Case: Same as abdomen, tied back as loop, then pulled forward.

Hackle: Blue Dun Tied Parachute. Oversize.

Thorax: Dubbed Muskrat or any Grey Dubbing. Note: try a few wraps of Larva Lace Dry Fly foam in front of post before dubbing.

Eyes: Same piece as wing case after loop is pulled forward and clipped.

Marking Pen: Permanent black felt tip.

Step 1. Start thread and cover forward ½ of hook shank.

Step 2. Tie in tip of braided mono half way between the midpoint of the shank and the eye. This is the center of the thread cover area. Hold mono on top of hook and wrap thread back to middle of shank.

Step 3. Use permanent marker to stripe abdomen. Stripes should be approximately ¹/₁₆″. More blue should show than black. Cut off mono approx. equal to twice the length of the entire hook.

Step 4. Tie in a loop of braided mono by the tips, just in front of the tip of the abdomen.

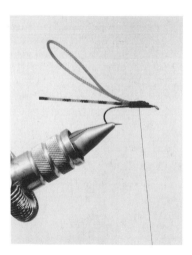

Step 5. Loop should reach back to the end of the abdomen. Wrap thread back over loop to middle of shank. Raise loop up and forward, then thread wrap a post around the base of the loop in preparation for a parachute hackle.

Step 6. To insure floatability – place 2 wraps of dry fly foam directly in front of the post. Make the wraps on top of each other. Trim off excess. Leave thread behind the post.

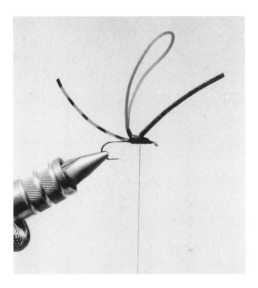

Step 7. Select blue dun hackle and strip off hackle fibers from the base. Do not cut off excess quill. With the tip of the hackle forward – tie in quill behind the base of the loop. The excess quill provides an easy handle for this. Trim off excess quill. The hackle is intentionally over-sized, 2 gaps or more. Do not wrap hackle.

Step 8. Sparse dub muskrat onto thread. Too much dubbing causes too large a thorax. Wrap dubbing behind the post to cover thread then forward of post ½ way to hook eye. Don't forget to lift the hackle up and out of the way.

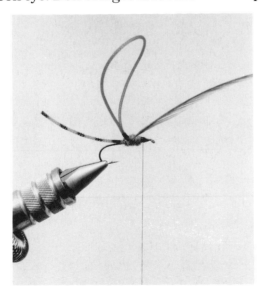

Step 9. Wrap parachute hackle around the post counter-clockwise. Leave enough hackle tip to tie off in front of the dubbing.

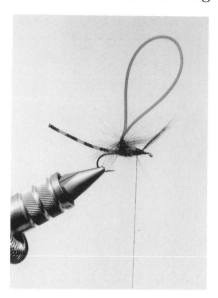

Step 10. To eliminate drop off and keep the mono loop tie down from sliding to the eye of the hook, wrap thread from the hook eye back to dubbing then back to hook. Roll hackle and mono loop back lightly while doing this to prevent tying down hackle fibers.

Step 11. With one hand – pull hackle fibers back out of the way while the other hand brings the mono loop forward and down until the parachute hackle is parallel to the hook shank. Pass thread over the mono loop 4 or 5 times with the vise hand. Raise loop with free hand should thread start slipping forward. Change hands and place several wraps under the mono loop to anchor. Trim off trapped hackle fibers.

Step 12. Cut the loop and figure eight the thread between the strands of mono to secure and hold slightly flared.

Step 13. Whip finish and cut off thread. Trim mono strands to slightly longer than the hook eye. Mark tips of mono with felt tip marker. Place head cement on head of fly, tips of mono and the tip of the abdomen to prevent fraying. Clear throat and hook eye of cement unless this fly is for a relative or a friend that always insists on freebies.

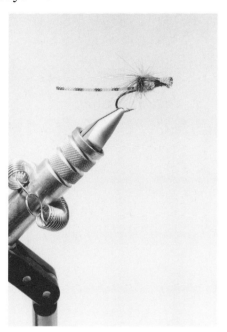

AQUATIC EARTHWORM
(Annelida, Oligochaeta)

These are generally elongated, cylindrical worms that are usually 1-30 mm but sometimes well over 100 mm in length. Body segmented, 7-500 segments, and typically bears a few short bristles or hair. Color is variable.

Of the segmented worms (phylum Annelida), the earth worms (class Oligochaeta) are one of the groups that are well represented in fresh water environments. Although most are poorly known, there may be 200 species or more in North America. Most aquatic earthworms may be found in silky substrates and among the debris and detritus of pounds, lakes, pools, streams, and rivers. Some are associated with algalmats, some are amphibious and still others may be generally confined to marginal wet environments.

McCafferty: *Aquatic Entomology* ©1983 Boston: Jones and Bartlett Publishers.

These worms are better known to the fly fisherman as the San Juan Worm. This Annelido has only taken national recognition in the past five or six years, but has been a closely guarded pattern for many. There are a number of patterns that represent this critter, I will introduce you to a few.

THE SAN JUAN WORM — Plate #13, Fly #2
   Hook: Mustad 7958. Size 8-12
   Thread: 6/0 Uni-thread
   Body: Micro or Ultra Chenille
   Color: Red, Burgundy, Amber, Red-Brown, Tan, Black

Step 1. Attach thread to hook then attach the chenille leaving approximately one and a half times the hook length as a tail.

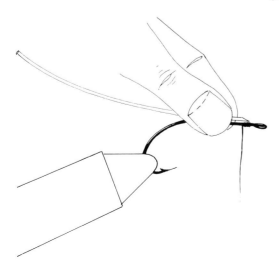

Step 2. Bring tying thread ³/₄ of the way up the hook shank. Then, wrap the chenille 3 to 4 wraps and tie down leaving one and a half times the hook length as the front section.

Step 3. Whip finish and detach the flying thread.

Step 4. Using a match or cigarette lighter, singe each end of the chenille creating a slight taper.

This is a pattern that my good friend Colonel Daack calls a "No Brainer."

LARGE SAN JUAN WORM — Plate #13, Fly #1
Hook: Mustad 94720. Size 4-8
Body: Ultra Chenille
Color: Red, Burgundy, Amber, Red-Brown, Tan, Black
Thread: 6/0 Uni-thread

Step 1. Bend the hook shank to a large arcing configuration.

Step 2. Attach the thread just above the point of the hook.

Step 3. Attach the ultra chenille leaving approximately one-half the hook length extending off the back. Then bring the thread forward to within one eye width of the hook eye

Step 4. Using close tight wraps, wrap the chenille forward to the thread.

Step 5. Tie off the chenille and whip finish leaving approximately the same amount in front as left off the back.

Step 6. Singe taper on each end.

Note: This worm can be tied as long as three inches.

SAN JUAN (HARD WORM) — Plate #13, Fly #7
   Hook: Mustad 37140. Size 4-10
   Body: Larva Lace Body Material or Nymph Rib
   Thread: 6/0 — Red Uni-thread

Step 1. Place hook in vise and bend the shank up, creating a more gradual
   curve. Take out at least ½ of its original bend.

Step 2. Attach thread just behind the eye of the hook.

Step 3. Cut a four inch piece of orange Larva Lace body material. Trim one end
   to a 45 degree angle.

Step 4. Attach the angled end of the lace just behind the eye of the hook.

Step 5. Pull the larva lace directly over the back of the hook and wrap tightly
   over it with bright red thread. Continue stretching the lace while wrapping
   bring the thread all the way to the back of the hook.

Step 6. Now, bring the tying thread back to the eye of the hook making the
   shank completely red.

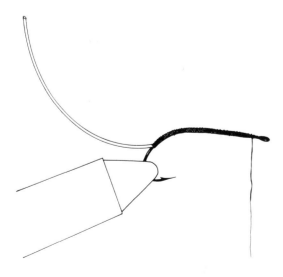

Step 7. Using the conventional wrap technique bring the larva lace body material up the shank and tie down at the eye.

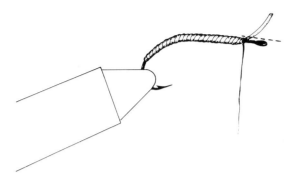

Step 8. Make six wraps when tying down the lace then stretch the material forward. Snip the lace off and the end will pull back to the tie off area.

Step 9. Form small red head and whip finish.

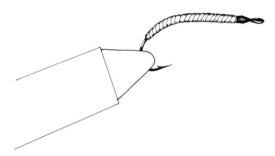

Step 10. Remove the barb on this hook. It has a tendency of hooking on the upper part of the mouth. By removing the barb, the chances of hurting your fish when extracting the hook are decreased.

THE AQUATIC EARTHWORM — Plate #13, Fly #4

The tying procedures for the earth worm are exactly the same as the San Juan Hard Worm except that between Steps 6 and 7 tie in two wraps of white thin Larva Lace dry fly foam as a collar. This collar should be down 1/3 the length of the hook.

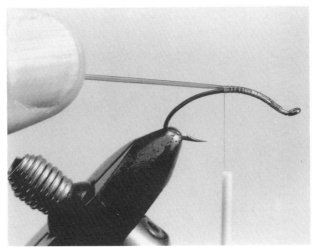

Tying on Larva Lace

Tying in foam

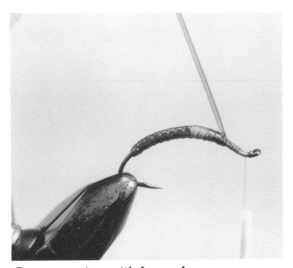

Overwrapping with Larva Lace

When the collar is tied in, pick up from Step 7 and complete the fly using red-brown larva lace body material and brown thread.

CLOUDY DAY WORM — Plate #13, Fly #5

Same as San Juan Hard Worm except tie with a piece of pearlescent crystal hair inserted into shrimp colored (#12) Larva Lace body material.

GLOBUG-EGG PATTERN

What has happened to fly fishing? If this fly had to be put into a category it would fall in with the San Juan Worm. That's because its productivity level is equal, plus it took me a long time to accept it as a kosher pattern.

While originally used by steel headers, the tail water and lake run trout fishers have finally adopted it. The egg pattern flys are also on the top of the list of fishermen fly fishing for KoKonee Salmon. In the fall, during the salmon's upstream journey, fly rodders fish the egg just off the bottom with a natural drift because the spawning salmon are trailed by gorging trout. Your chances are high of catching a trophy size fish with the egg.

GLOBUG EGG — Plate #8, Flies 13 & 15

Materials:

Hook: Mustad 9174. Sizes: 4-8

Thread: 3/0 Monocore or Fine Translucent

Body: Globug Yarn. Popular colors are peach, florescent pink, florescent orange, and chartreuse.

Step 1. Attach tying thread in the middle of the hook shank.

Step 2. Cut four pieces of Glo Bug yarn 1 1/2 inches long.

Step 3. Place the yarn pieces together lengthwise and attach them to the hook.

    A. Position the yarn lengthwise on the hook.
    B. Make three top pressure wraps to secure the yarn.
    C. Pick up the yarn between your fingers and wrap three more wraps of thread in front and three more behind the yarn.
    D. Whip finish and detach the thread.

Step 4. Again, hold the yarn straight up between your fingers and clip it off the distance of the hook gap above the shank. When clipping the yarn, clip in an arcing motion rather than straight across.

Step 5. The Glo Bug yarn should spread out and around the hook forming a small puff ball. Don't be afraid to help the material spread out with your fingers after it is clipped.

Tips: Globug – Egg Fly

1. If your first egg does not come out the way you wanted keep trying and check the following:

    A. Make sure your yarn did not spin under the hook while tying down.

    B. If you feel you need a stronger thread, try Kevlar.

    C. When you see all the clippings you'll feel you waste more than you use. Save the clippings and use them for dubbing material.

    D. When tying an egg with a small colored dot in it, just lay a thin piece of different color Bug yarn on top of the bunch before tying the yarn down to the hook.

THE DOUBLE EGG — Plate #8, Fly #14

Hook: Mustad 3906B. Size-10-14

Body: Glo Bug Yarn

Thread: Larva Lace Translucent – Fine

Egg Sack Imitation: White Marabou or White Glo Bug Yarn

This egg is tied identically to the standard Glo Bug except there are two eggs on the hook instead of one. One variation that some fishermen have been using is the tying of white marabou or Glo Bug yarn in the front to simulate the White Sticky Eggsack.

This pattern fishes very well as a dropper. The Double Egg pattern has been used by steelheaders for many years, but in its original form as the Babine Special.

Closing Comments from Author

I hope that this book has provided you with a few tips to aid in your tying. The materials and techniques in fly tying are growing and changing so fast that keeping current on every aspect is a next to impossible challenge.

One frustrating part of writing a book of this kind is knowing that some topics were being overlooked. What I have tried to do is just give a general overview of the many techniques and materials currently in use in the field. There are always more techniques and materials which deserve consideration than time and space to describe them. As fly tyers, all we can hope to do is enjoy the art of tying and help promote it by sharing with other tyers.

Anglers today are truly fortunate because of the large number of excellent books on the market. To try and list them all would mean adding more chapters to this book. What I would rather do is suggest that you contact your local fly fishing shop and review the many books available there. If you have no such resource available to you, try contacting some of the people on the list below to help you out.

For your interest in this book, I thank you.

Editor, *American Angler & Fly Tyer*
P.O. Box 280
Intervale, NH 03845

Editor, *Fly Fisherman*
P.O. Box 8200
Harrisburg, PA 17105

Editor, *Fly Fishing*
P.O. Box 82112
Portland, OR 97282

Editor, *Fly Rod & Reel*
P.O. Box 370
Camden, ME 04856

Index